THE FUNNY PAGES

Other books edited by Judy Brown

Joke Soup

Joke Stew

THE FUNNY PAGES

1,473 Jokes from
Today's Funniest Comedians

EDITED BY

Judy Brown

**Andrews McMeel
Publishing**

Kansas City

02 03 04 05 06 RR4 10 9 8 7 6 5 4 3 2 1

ISBN: 0-7407-2686-2

Library of Congress Control Number: 2002103642

JudyBrowni@usa.net

Book design and composition by Kelly & Company

Acknowledgments

First and foremost, I hafta thank the comedians and other succinct wits whose words, and the specific way they arrange them, make up this book.

And then I must acknowledge Jean Lucas and Andrews McMeel for slapping those words between such slaphappy covers; Sandy Choron, who mopped up that laughing matter of a contract; HBO and Comedy Central, which supply tons of comedy fun at digital cable prices; the comedy clubs that, with the help of the two-drink minimum, keep us all delightfully light-headed while laughing; and my comedy students, who teach me as much about writing jokes as I teach them.

And let us not forget Felix and Oscar, two orange cats born while I was bond slave on a sitcom, who have faithfully slept fifteen hours a day while I edited three joke books.

Abortion

Accidents

These guys say they're against abortion because birth is a miracle. Popcorn is a miracle, too, if you don't know how it's done.

☎ .... **Elayne Boosler**

I broke my arm trying to fold a bed. It wasn't the kind that folds.

☎ .... **Steven Wright**

A man at a tool-and-die company died today when he was hit by a tool.

☎ .... **George Carlin**

If life begins at conception, why can't you declare your unborn child as a tax deduction?

☎ .... **Caryn Leschen**

You saw that report about traffic accidents being caused by drivers nodding off. The last thing they hear is, "Now, a medley by Kenny G."

☎ .... **David Letterman**

> *If abortions are outlawed, only outlaws will have abortions.*
>
> ☎   **Steve Carell**

Acupuncture

Acupuncture works on the principle of distraction. You're not going to feel the arthritis in your knee when someone's ramming a butterfly-specimen needle into the nape of your neck. It's the same reason your nose never itches when your ankle is caught in a bear trap.

☎ . . . . **Dennis Miller**

A friend of mine is into Voodoo Acupuncture. You don't even have to go. You'll just be walking down the street, and ... *aaaahhhhhh,* that's *much* better.

☎ . . . . **Steven Wright**

Do you think that every time someone has acupuncture there's a voodoo doll out there having a really bad day?

☎ . . . . **Caryn Leschen**

Advertising

The ad in the paper said "Big Sale. Last Week!" Why advertise? I already missed it. They're just rubbing it in.

☎ . . . . **Yakov Smirnoff**

SUVs are named for exotic places we'll never go, like the Dodge Durango or the GMC Yukon. There should be truth in advertising: like calling them the Dodge Dubuque, or the GMC "I'm Going to 7-Eleven for a Moon Pie."

☎ . . . . **Daryl Hogue**

The biggest marketing disaster in history was Campbell's Soup for One. They might as well have called it Cream of Loser Soup. "Open can. Add tears."

☎ . . . . **Traci Skene**

People for the Ethical Treatment of Animals spokesmodels such as Pamela Anderson, Melissa Etheridge, and actress Dominique Swain have all appeared nude in ads for the organization. Which is all part of PETA's plan to ensure that people viewing the posters would have no recollection as to what the advertisements were actually for.

☎ . . . . **Jon Stewart**

Wal-Mart is producing its own brand of wines. So you have to ask yourself, "Does green go with fish?" Their slogan is "We put the 'sewer' in *connosewer.*" Have you seen their ads? "Rent on trailer, $15. Cough syrup to put kids to sleep, $3. Wal-Mart wine, $2. An evening of trailer park romance, priceless."

☎ . . . . **Jay Leno**

Miller Beer is doing openly gay ads. The guys are using coasters.

☎ . . . . **Craig Kilborn**

Advice

Never comment on a woman's rear end. Never use the words "large" or "size" with "rear end." Never. Avoid the area altogether. Trust me.

☎ . . . . **Tim Allen**

Never moon a werewolf.

☎ . . . . **Mike Binder**

Put kitty litter in your shoes, and it'll take away the odor. Unless, of course, you own a cat.

☎ . . . . **Jay Leno**

Aging

I have the body of an eighteen-year-old. I keep it in the fridge.

☎ . . . . **Spike Milligan**

I can tell I'm getting older, because I find myself using words like "spacious," "roomy," and "comfortable" when I'm buying underwear.

☎ . . . . **Reno Goodale**

At age thirty our bodies are supposedly slowing down. I don't see that, unless what slows down first is my ability to notice things.

☎ . . . . **Al Lubel**

After thirty, a body has a mind of its own.

☎ . . . . **Bette Midler**

Thirty-five is when you finally get your head together, and your body starts falling apart.

☎ . . . . **Caryn Leschen**

I'm 482 months old; can you tell I'm a new father?

☎ **Reno Goodale**

One trouble with growing older is that it gets progressively tougher to find a famous historical figure who didn't amount to much when he was your age.

☎ . . . . **Bill Vaughan**

I'm forty-nine years old; that's 72,000 in frequent-flier miles.

☎ . . . . **Danny Liebert**

I recently turned fifty, which is young for a tree, midlife for an elephant, and ancient for a quarter-miler, whose son now says, "Dad, I just can't run the quarter with you anymore unless I bring something to read."

☎ . . . . **Bill Cosby**

Middle age is when your age starts to show around your middle.

☎ . . . . **Bob Hope**

I don't plan to grow old gracefully. I plan to have facelifts until my ears meet.

☎ . . . . **Rita Rudner**

What I look forward to is continued immaturity followed by death.

☎ . . . . **Dave Barry**

First you forget names, then you forget faces. Next you forget to pull your zipper up. And finally, you forget to pull it down.

☎ . . . . **George Burns**

It's no longer a question of staying healthy. It's a question of finding a sickness you like.

☎ **Jackie Mason**

I don't feel old. I don't feel anything till noon. That's when it's time for my nap.

☎ . . . . **Bob Hope**

How young can you die of old age?

☎ . . . . **Steven Wright**

The other day at an Australian track meet, a 101-year-old man ran a mile and set a world record for people over 100 years old. There is some controversy concerning the record, though, because when the man began the race he was only 98.

☎ . . . . **Conan O'Brien**

According to the oldest person in the world, a 121-year-old French woman, the secret to long life is to start every day with a little bit of olive oil. That's not new, Popeye's been doing that for years.

☎ . . . . **Jay Leno**

He is so old that his blood type was discontinued.

☎ . . . . **Bill Dana**

The oldest man in the world passed away yesterday at the age of 112. The cause of death, say doctors ... was being 112.

☎ .... **Conan O'Brien**

Air-Conditioning

I turned my air conditioner the other way around, and it got cold outside. The weatherman said, "I don't understand it. It was supposed to be 80 degrees today," and I thought, "OOPS."

☎ .... **Steven Wright**

Alcohol

I hate the cliché "Alcohol's a crutch." I've never seen anyone with a broken ankle admire their crutches and say, "These things make me more confident and witty!" Or a drinker lament, "Dude, I'd love to go out. But the doctor says I have to stay on beer for six weeks. It sucks!"

☎ .... **Adam Gropman**

An Arizona brewer has come out with a new "chili" beer. It's essentially beer flavored with chili. Now, who exactly is this for? People who feel they're not spending enough time in the restroom?

☎ .... **Jay Leno**

The federal government is considering a proposal that would update the warning label on beer and other alcoholic beverages. For instance, one of the new warnings says, "Caution: Excessive drinking could cause karaoke."

☎ .... **Conan O'Brien**

The first purpose of alcohol is to make English your second language. You may be a Nobel Prize physicist, but after nine, ten Heinekens you're speaking fluent Drunken-ese. Next thing you know, you have a friend in a headlock, "I love ya, I love ya, that's the kinda love I have for you, goddamn it."

☎ .... **Robin Williams**

A Dutch food and liquor maker is introducing an ice cream spiked with alcohol. Finally, a product that will destroy your liver and raise your cholesterol at the same time.

☎ .... **Jay Leno**

There are new lemonade liquor drinks aimed at kids. And now Gerbers has come out with Strained Banana Daiquiris.

☎ .... **Jon Stewart**

Ambulances

In some parts of the country ambulances' response times are so slow, the best thing to do is call for a pizza and get the driver to drop you off at the hospital on the way back.

☎ .... **Don MacLean**

I don't get no respect. The time I got hurt, on the way to the hospital the ambulance stopped for gas.

☎ . . . . . **Rodney Dangerfield**

I was in front of an ambulance the other day, and I noticed that the word *ambulance* was spelled in reverse print on the hood. I thought, "Well, isn't that clever," in the rear-view mirror, I can read the word *ambulance* behind me. Of course, while you're reading, you don't see where you're going, you crash, you need an ambulance. I think they're just trying to drum up some business on the way back from lunch.

☎ . . . . **Jerry Seinfeld**

Amusement Parks

Six Flags just had their billionth visitor. When they asked the man what he'd do with his prize money, he said, "I'm going to Disney World."

☎ . . . . **Jay Leno**

Animals

All creatures must learn to coexist. That's why the brown bear and the field mouse can share their lives, and live in harmony. Of course they can't mate, or the mice would explode.

☎ . . . . **Betty White**

To control the deer population, game wardens are shooting deer with contraceptive darts in New York. Now they're thinking of expanding the program to the NBA.

☎ .... **Jay Leno**

How many of those dead animals you see on the highway are suicides?

☎ **Dennis Miller**

My parents used to take me to the pet department and tell me it was a zoo.

☎ .... **Billy Connolly**

Size isn't everything. The whale is endangered, while the ant continues to do just fine.

☎ .... **Bill Vaughan**

Dogs feel very strongly that they should always go with you in the car, in case the need should arise for them to bark violently at nothing right in your ear.

☎ .... **Dave Barry**

Scientists believe that monkeys can be taught to think, lie, and even play politics within their community. If we can just teach them to cheat on their wives we can save millions on congressional salaries.

☎ .... **Jay Leno**

The other day when I was walking through the woods, I saw a rabbit standing in front of a candle making shadows of people on a tree.

☎ .... **Steven Wright**

Animals have two functions in today's society, to be delicious and to fit well.

☎ . . . . **Greg Proops**

In China panda sperm is being collected for artificial insemination. Unsolicited donations were made by twelve guys in panda suits.

☎ . . . . **Jon Stewart**

I love a dog. He does nothing for political reasons.

☎ . . . . **Will Rogers**

I love animals, but they don't love me. This is what I hear, "Fluffy never bit anyone before!" Look for me on the new fall show, "When Parakeets Attack."

☎ . . . . **Dobie Maxwell**

Answering Machines

Have you ever called someone, and you're disappointed when they answer? "Uh, I didn't know you were there, I just wanted to leave a message, 'Sorry I missed you.'" What you have is people who don't want to talk, and the phone machine is this respirator keeping marginal, brain-dead relationships alive. Because when we come home we want to see that little flashing red light and go, "All right, messages!" It's very important for human beings to feel they are popular amongst a large group of people they have no interest in.

☎ . . . . **Jerry Seinfeld**

I like to leave a message before the beep.

☎ . . . . **Steven Wright**

Aptitude

When I finished school, I took one of those career aptitude tests, and based on my verbal ability score, they suggested I become a mime.

☎ . . . . **Tim Cavanagh**

Architecture

My house is made out of balsa wood. When no one is home across the street except the little kids, I lift my house up over my head. I tell them to stay out of my yard, or I'll throw it at them.

☎ . . . . **Steven Wright**

Astrology

My wife's an earth sign. I'm a water sign. Together we make mud.

☎ . . . . **Henny Youngman**

Astronomy

Interestingly, according to modern astronomers, space is finite. This is a very comforting thought, particularly for people who cannot remember where they left things.

☎ . . . . **Woody Allen**

Authority

I'm always getting screwed by the system. That's my lot in life. I'm the system's bitch.

☎ . . . . **Drew Carey**

When authorities warn you of the sinfulness of sex, there is an important lesson to be learned: Do not have sex with the authorities.

☎ . . . . **Matt Groening**

Babies

When I was born, I was so surprised I couldn't talk for a year and a half.

☎ . . . . **Gracie Allen**

When I was a baby, I kept a diary. Recently I was re-reading it. It said: "Day One: Still tired from the move. Day Two: Everybody talks to me like I'm an idiot."

☎ . . . . **Steven Wright**

There's a lot to do when you have a baby. The first thing, which is taking me a really long time, I have to figure out who the father is.

☎ . . . . **Heidi Joyce**

Naming our kid was a real trial. I seize up when I have to name a document on my computer. I didn't name my son after me. What if he turns into a maniac? How'd you like to be Jeffrey Dahmer Sr.?

☎ . . . . **Jeff Stilson**

That was a big deal, you're pregnant and trying to come up with names for your kid. My husband's family is Jewish, so they name everybody in their family for dead people. Which I respect, but it's kind of annoying since they have these names that probably killed these people in the first place. And my family is basically Irish hillbillies from Appalachia, so we usually name our kids after two, three shots of bourbon.

☎ . . . . **Stephanie Hodge**

The hardest thing in the world is making a kid happy after he's been circumcised.

☎ . . . . **Damon Wayans**

What's tough about seeing people when they have a new baby is that you have to try and match their level of enthusiasm. They're always so excited. Just once I would like to meet a couple that goes, "You know, we're not that happy with him, frankly. I think we really made a big mistake. We should've gotten an aquarium. You want him? We've had enough."

☎ . . . . **Jerry Seinfeld**

Studies show rectal thermometers are still the best way to take a baby's temperature. Plus, it really shows them who's boss.

☎ **Tina Fey**

I like flipping through my mom's photo albums. I enjoy seeing what I looked like as a baby, and what my apartment furniture looked like new.

☎ .... **Jeff Shaw**

Heinz is coming out with a baby bottle shaped like a woman's breast. They should sell beer in it; they'd make a fortune.

☎ .... **Jay Leno**

Baby-Sitters

When you're a parent, you're a prisoner of war. You can't go anywhere without paying someone to come and look after your kids. In the old days, baby-sitters were fifty cents an hour; they'd steam-clean the carpet and detail your car. Now they've got their own union. I couldn't afford it, so I had my mother come over. The sitters called her a scab and beat her up on the front lawn.

☎ .... **Robert G. Lee**

They say you should video-tape your baby-sitter, but I don't think you should involve your kid in a sting operation.

☎ .... **Dave Chappelle**

I don't have a baby, but I still book a baby-sitter. I tell her to check on the kid after a half hour or so. Then when I return I go, "Escaped?! Well, give me fifty bucks, and we'll call it even."

☎ .... **Harry Hill**

My fiancé wanted a bachelor party, but I said no way. Guys always claim, "That's my last night of freedom." I don't think so. Your last night of freedom was the one *before* you proposed.

☎ .... **Denise Robb**

Bachelor Parties

I have a friend who is about to get married. They're having the bachelor party and the bridal shower the same day. So it's conceivable that while the girl's friends are giving her sexy lingerie, the guy could be at a nude bar watching a table dancer in the exact same outfit. I think that'll be a very special moment.

☎ .... **Jerry Seinfeld**

I threw my best friend a bachelorette party. I could say I did this for her last night of freedom. But frankly, after a year of fielding really important bride crises like "Jordan almonds or white chocolate–covered cashews?" I've earned three pitchers of margaritas and a naked blue-collar worker.

☎ .... **Kelly Maguire**

Bad Breath

We should have a way of telling people they have bad breath without hurting their feelings. "Well, I'm bored. Let's go brush our teeth." Or, "I've got to make a phone call, hold this gum in your mouth."

☎ . . . . **Brad Stine**

Baking

How come if you mix flour and water together you get glue? And when you add eggs and sugar, you get a cake? Where does the glue go?

☎ . . . . **Rita Rudner**

A ninety-year-old woman in Oregon has won all the state's baking prizes. Martha Stewart sent her a telegram today saying, "You're going down, bitch."

☎ . . . . **Craig Kilborn**

Banks

Bank of America laid off thirteen thousand workers. The lines at the bank were too short.

☎ . . . . **Jay Leno**

Basketball

If Kobe Bryant had a kidney stone, would he pass it?

☎ . . . . **Jay Leno**

Men own basketball teams. Every year cheerleaders' outfits get tighter and briefer, and players' shorts get baggier and longer.

☎ .... **Rita Rudner**

The NBA's Washington Bullets will be changing their name to avoid being associated with an image of crime. So from now on, they're just going to be known as the Bullets.

☎ .... **Jay Leno**

Basketball legend Michael Jordan denied reports that he was making a comeback. The good news is that Jordan's cologne also won't be making a comeback.

☎ .... **Conan O'Brien**

My parents sent me to basketball fantasy camp. I got to sleep in the same bed with Patrick Ewing. Except I like a fan, and the noise kept him awake.

☎ .... **Adam Sandler**

Seventy-six couples got married at a Philadelphia 76ers game. Shaquille O'Neal threw rice at the couples and missed every one.

☎ .... **Craig Kilborn**

Beauty Pageants

The Miss America pageant is considering adding an academic competition, where contestants have to answer multiple-choice questions about history. Which means it may actually be harder to become Miss America than it is to become the president of the United States.

☎ . . . . Conan O'Brien

What I think is so dangerous about beauty pageants is the very narrow scope of what they regard as beautiful. Society in general's idea of beautiful has much too much to do with thin. My feeling is that when you can actually see a woman digesting, she's too thin.

☎ . . . . Jonathan Katz

That Miss America pageant, the talent competition is tough. Miss New York, using only a coat hanger, can break into a Lexus, and the entire time she's smoking.

☎ . . . . David Letterman

How is it in this country that, if you pore over the *Sports Illustrated* swimsuit issue, you're a pervert, but if you ogle the same babes in alphabetical order by state, you're patriotic?

☎ . . . . Bill Maher

A beauty queen in Thailand was disqualified when he turned out to be a man. The judges should have been suspicious, since his talent was peeing standing up.

☎ . . . . Conan O'Brien

Birth

In the natural childbirth classes my wife and I took, the birthing process was represented by a hand puppet being pushed through a sock. So at the actual birth I was shocked to see all this blood. The thing I had prepared myself for was a lot of lint.

☎ .... **Steve Skrovan**

I envy the kangaroo. That pouch setup is extraordinary; the baby crawls out of the womb when it is about two inches long, gets into the pouch, and proceeds to mature. I'd have a baby if it would develop in my handbag.

☎ .... **Rita Rudner**

They call us "coaches." The job is to remind your wife to breathe. You realize exactly how worthless I am in this thing? When was the last time you had to be reminded to breathe? It's like saying, "Digest!"

☎ .... **Robert Klein**

We delivered our child by natural childbirth, the procedure invented by a man named Lamaze, the Marquis de Lamaze, a disciple of Dr. Josef Mengele, who concluded that women could counteract the incredible pain of childbirth by breathing. That's like asking a man to tolerate a vasectomy by hyperventilating.

☎ .... **Dennis Wolfberg**

We planned this beautiful, totally natural, unmedicated delivery. What kind of stupid-ass idea is that? Next time I want the epidural at the moment of conception. Numb for nine months.

☎ . . . . **Heidi Joyce**

I once heard two ladies going on and on about the pains of childbirth and how men don't seem to know what real pain is. I asked if either of them ever got themselves caught in a zipper.

☎ . . . . **Emo Philips**

A sixty-two-year-old French woman has given birth. It's smart to wait. There's no day care expense if you don't have kids until you retire.

☎ . . . . **Jay Leno**

Having a child is surely the most beautiful irrational act that two people in love can commit.

☎ . . . . **Bill Cosby**

Birthdays

There comes a time when you should stop expecting other people to make a big deal about your birthday. That time is age eleven.

☎ . . . . **Dave Barry**

Why is it that with birthday cakes you can blow on them and spit on them and every-one rushes to get a piece?

☎ . . . . **Bobby Kelton**

On my sixteenth birthday my parents tried to surprise me with a car, but they missed.

☎ . . . . **Tom Cotter**

Ray Charles was given a surprise party for his seventieth birthday. His friends all jumped out from behind, well, nothing.

☎ . . . . **Craig Kilborn**

You know what Bo Diddley got for his birthday? Diddley squat.

☎ . . . . **Jay Leno**

Books

If you read a lot of books, you're considered well-read. But if you watch a lot of TV, you're not considered well-viewed.

☎ . . . . **Lily Tomlin**

I buy books on suicide at bookstores. You can't get them at the library, because people don't return them.

☎ . . . . **Kevin Nealon**

I recently bought a book of free verse. For twelve dollars.

☎ . . . . **George Carlin**

A Texas town has banned the Harry Potter books because they glorify magic, and learning to read.

☎ . . . . **Craig Kilborn**

A bookstore is one of the only pieces of evidence we have that people are still thinking.

☎ . . . . **Jerry Seinfeld**

A woman has written a book claiming she was married to Bob Dylan for six years. The marriage wasn't really a secret, but when Dylan told people about it they couldn't understand what he was saying.

☎ . . . . **Conan O'Brien**

Here's a book called *Keys to Inner Simplicity*. Take a leak in a rental car. Sleep with the baby-sitter. Kick a shoe sales-man in the nuts.

☎ . . . . **David Letterman**

Stephen King has written a letter to his fans that he's repeating himself too much and is going to retire from writing novels. The letter is five hundred pages long and ends with a bucket of blood being tossed onto a possessed car.

☎ . . . . **Craig Kilborn**

Boxing

Like all men, I like to watch sports, but I'm still trying to figure out boxing. That's a big tough man's masculine sport. But you know what the prize money is called in a heavyweight boxing match? A purse. The two biggest, baddest men in the world fighting for a purse. A purse and a belt.

☎ . . . . **Mike Dugan**

Boxing gyms are still pretty much a man's domain, but now some women are stepping into the ring and onto the canvas. I don't get it. Doesn't it hurt? Damn straight it hurts. It's a man's place to pretend something doesn't hurt.

☎ .... **Tim Allen**

Mike Tyson says he's going to retire from boxing and go back to his first love, beating up people for free.

☎ .... **Craig Kilborn**

Officials are saying that Tyson has tarnished the sport of boxing. Don King is furious, "Hey, that's my job!"

☎ **Bill Maher**

Imagine a Pulitzer Prize fighter.

☎ .... **Steven Wright**

Breakups

There is one thing I would break up over, and that is if she caught me with another woman. I wouldn't stand for that.

☎ .... **Steve Martin**

I found my wife in bed naked one day next to a Vietnamese guy and a black guy. I took a picture and sent it to Benetton. You never know.

☎ .... **Franck Dubosc**

A woman broke up with me and sent me pictures of her and her new boyfriend in bed together. Solution? I sent them to her dad.

☎ . . . . **Christopher Case**

The hardest thing about getting out of a relationship is listening to the radio. Because every song is about being in love, or being heartbroken. And I found that the only song I was comfortable with is that Peter, Paul, and Mary song, "If I Had a Hammer."

☎ . . . . **Ellen DeGeneres**

A former girlfriend remembers Bill Gates as having bad breath. He remembers her as not having $100 billion.

☎ . . . . **Conan O'Brien**

I spotted my ex-boyfriend at the mall. We had a really bad breakup, and I didn't want to make eye contact with him. Thank God I've had years of waitress training.

☎ . . . . **Kate Mason**

My ex-girlfriend was very sexy. She reminded me of the Sphinx because she was very mysterious and eternal and solid, and her nose was shot off by French soldiers.

☎ . . . . **Emo Philips**

Breast-Feeding

My mother breast-fed me with powdered milk. It was my first real do-it-yourself project.

☎ . . . . **Buzz Nutley**

Women breast-feeding in public always defend themselves by saying, "It's a beautiful thing." Yeah, so is sex, but I've never done it in the middle of Denny's. Although that at least would be a Grand Slam Breakfast.

☎ . . . . **Traci Skene**

A woman was in court because she's still breast-feeding her five-year-old kid. And you thought you were embarrassed when your mom brought your lunch to school.

☎ . . . . **Jay Leno**

A child is too old to breast-feed when he can unhook Mommy's bra with one hand.

☎ . . . . **Anthony Clark**

Budgets

I've been budgeting recently. I'm putting aside half of my paycheck each month for coffee and cigarettes. I know I shouldn't complain, but if you buy yourself a pack of cigarettes and throw in a latte from Starbucks, that's the equivalent of round-trip airfare.

☎ . . . . **Cindee Weiss**

Buttonholes

I lost a buttonhole today.

☎ . . . . **Steven Wright**

Camping

Camping is nature's way of promoting the motel business.

☎ .... **Dave Barry**

Jews don't go camping. Life is hard enough as it is.

☎ .... **Carol Siskind**

Cars

I put a new engine in my car but didn't take the old one out. Now my car goes five hundred miles an hour.

☎ .... **Steven Wright**

The best car safety device is a rear-view mirror with a cop in it.

☎ .... **Dudley Moore**

I've never known a man who wasn't deeply attached on a very emotional level to his beloved vehicle. Whether it was a piece of junk or a masterpiece made no difference. They rode in their metal boxes and were in control of their lives. I think I know why so many men are afraid to make a commitment to women. It's because we can't be steered.

☎ .... **Rita Rudner**

My aunt, thirty years a feminist, says, "A car is just an extension of your penis." Oh, I *wish*.

☎ .... **Tim Allen**

Jaguar recalled 3,500 cars. But they were quick to point out that the problem is strictly with emissions and has nothing to do with the vehicle's main function, getting bald, middle-aged guys laid.

☎ . . . . **Bill Maher**

They're working on cars powered by fuel made from beans. You think you hate getting stuck behind a bus now?

☎ . . . . **Jay Leno**

I don't know anything about automobile repairs. If you ask me to fix a car, it's like asking Ray Charles to drive it.

☎ . . . . **Robert Murray**

I don't know much about auto mechanics, but there's no way I'm gonna admit that. "My car's making a noise, and I'm pretty sure it's the uh, carbolator . . . carbonator . . . carbonizer, the distribulator. I blew a brisket." And the mechanic says, "It's the emergency brake, you left it on."

☎ . . . . **Adam Gropman**

I hooked up my accelerator pedal in my car to my brake lights. I hit the gas, people behind me stop, and I'm gone.

☎ . . . . **Steven Wright**

GM announced that it no longer was going to produce the big cars: the Cadillac Fleetwood, Buick Roadmaster, Chevrolet Caprice have had all production stopped. Ford was going cancel production of the Lincoln Town Car but didn't because of religious reasons. As you know, the trunk of a Town Car is a mob burial ground.

☎ .... **Jay Leno**

A new-car dealership is a septic tank of desperation, suspicion, and loathing. The customers hate the dealers, the dealers hate the customers, the salespeople are all in competition with each other, and everyone assumes everyone else is lying. That new car smell? Nothing more than the purest distillation of basic human contempt.

☎ .... **Dennis Miller**

I passed a car dealership I looked in the window and I saw the most beautiful cars. And a fellow came out and said, "Come on in, they're bigger than ever and they last a lifetime!" He was talking about the payments.

☎ .... **Corbett Monica**

I saw a bumper sticker on a Mercedes that said, "I brake for tax shelters."

☎ .... **Nick Arnette**

The Pope's new Fiat doesn't have religious statues on the dashboard. Just a little mirror.

☎ .... **Jay Leno**

Casinos

Casino: Where you'll lose a hundred dollars in a slot machine and shrug your shoulders, then lose one dollar in a Coke machine and swear your head off.

☎ .... **Jeff Shaw**

In Boulder City, Nevada, the Gold Strike casino was destroyed by fire. Firefighters said they could have put the fire out sooner, but all the available water had already been used in the free drinks.

☎ .... **Jay Leno**

Cats

I've never understood why women love cats. Cats are independent, they don't listen, they don't come in when you call, they like to stay out all night, and when they're home they like to be left alone and sleep. In other words, every quality that women hate in a man, they love in a cat.

☎ .... **Jay Leno**

I had been told that the training procedure with cats was difficult. It's not. Mine had me trained in two days.

☎ .... **Bill Dana**

Cats are smarter than dogs. You can't get eight cats to pull a sled through snow.

☎ .... **Jeff Valdez**

No amount of time can erase the memory of a good cat, and no amount of masking tape can ever totally remove his fur from your couch.

☎ .... **Leo Dworken**

What if it was cats who invented technology: Would they have TV shows starring rubber squeak toys?

☎ .... **Douglas Coupland**

When a cat is dropped it always lands on its feet, and when toast is dropped it always lands with the buttered side down. I propose to strap buttered toast to the back of a cat; the two will hover, inches above the ground.

☎ .... **John Frazee**

Cats are intended to teach us that not everything in nature has a purpose.

☎ **Garrison Keillor**

Cats instinctively know the precise moment their owners will awaken, and then they wake them ten minutes sooner.

☎ .... **Jim Davis**

We have two cats. They're my wife's cats, Mischa and Alex. Women always have sensitive names for cats: Muffy, Fluffy, Buffy. Guys name cats things like Tuna Breath, Fur Face, Meow Head.

☎ .... **Larry Reeb**

The problem with cats is that they get the same exact look whether they see a moth or an ax murderer.

☎ .... **Paula Poundstone**

Cats always seem so very wise, when staring with their half-closed eyes. Can they be thinking, "I'll be nice, and maybe she will feed me twice"?

☎ .... **Bette Midler**

I love the way my cats stare at me. It's this long, penetrating, accusing glare like they've got some dirt on me. "I know you steal from work, I've seen the pens with the company name on them. Here are my demands: Fancy Feast only, no store brands, or I'm on the phone to management."

☎ .... **Andi Rhoads**

Celebrities

Pamela Anderson released a statement confirming that she had her breast implants removed. Doctors said that Pamela was doing fine and that her old implants are now dating Charlie Sheen.

☎ .... **Conan O'Brien**

You can't shame or humiliate modern celebrities. What used to be called shame and humiliation is now called publicity. And forget traditional character assassination. If you say a modern celebrity is an adulterer, a pervert, and a drug addict, all it means is that you've read his autobiography.

☎ . . . . **P. J. O'Rourke**

Gary Coleman was on trial, accused of punching a woman who asked him for an autograph. The judge ordered the woman to undergo a psychiatric exam to find out why the hell she was asking Gary Coleman for an autograph.

☎ . . . . **Jay Leno**

Leonardo DiCaprio may be getting sued because he hurled horse manure at the paparazzi while filming his latest movie. In his own defense, DiCaprio said, "That wasn't horse manure. That was the script for my latest movie."

☎ . . . . **Conan O'Brien**

Elvis was already pretty far gone by the time I first saw him. It made sense when women threw their bras at him. Obviously, he needed them.

☎ . . . . **Tom Kenny**

How big an Elvis fan am I? Just ask my sons, Tuinol and Seconal.

☎ **Dennis Miller**

Hugh Hefner now has seven girlfriends. One for each day of the week. Someone needs to tell him that those are nurses.

☎ .... **Jay Leno**

New York Yankee baseball player Derek Jeter was spotted at a restaurant making out with supermodel Tyra Banks. Unfortunately for Jeter, he was thrown out going for second base.

☎ .... **Conan O'Brien**

Bill Gates is the richest man in the world; his dog is number five. He has over ten million dollars in change sitting on his night stand.

☎ .... **Jay Leno**

Bill Gates is being sued by seven Microsoft employees who claim that the company discriminates against minorities. Apparently, at Microsoft, a minority is any employee who has a girlfriend.

☎ .... **Conan O'Brien**

Tonya Harding was drunk, playing video poker, and bashed her boyfriend with a hubcap. That's pretty much the white trash triple crown. Think how mad she must have been to pry a hubcap off her house. Actually, I'm surprised she threw it. It was part of her wedding china.

☎ .... **Jay Leno**

TV mogul Aaron Spelling turned seventy-four. Also turning seventy-four: crap.

☎ .... **Craig Kilborn**

A new biography of Madonna came out, and it lists all the men she's slept with. The book is called the Manhattan Telephone Directory.

☎ . . . . **Bill Maher**

Steven Segal is going to try a music career. He says he's only going to play what's in his head: rock music.

☎ . . . . **Jay Leno**

Vanilla Ice was arrested after police broke up a domestic dispute he was having with his wife about their telephone. Vanilla Ice was mad because his wife claimed the phone worked, even though it hadn't rung for five years.

☎ . . . . **Conan O'Brien**

O. J. Simpson says he can get any woman he wants. He must have bought a set of those throwing knives.

☎ . . . . **Jay Leno**

Charlie Sheen has just put his Malibu mansion on the market for 4.5 million dollars. Sheen's mansion comes with six bedrooms, three bathrooms, and Emilio Estevez.

☎ . . . . **Conan O'Brien**

Darryl Strawberry has entered a twelve-step program. The bad news is that he lives twelve steps from a crack house.

☎ . . . . **Jay Leno**

Ike Turner is single again. His thirteenth wife has left him. She came home unexpectedly and caught him punching out another woman.

☎ .... **Jay Leno**

No one in Hollywood dies anymore, they just become more marketable. I think that soon when a celebrity dies, they're just going to cremate them and roll them in to cigarettes. May as well. People would buy it. Soon you'll be able to go to 7-Eleven and buy two packs of 2Pac.

☎ .... **Brian Dowell**

Census

On my census form I listed a wife and three kids. I didn't want to look like a loser.

☎ .... **David Letterman**

The government says only 33 percent of Americans have returned their census forms. How do they know that?

☎ .... **Colin Quinn**

Change

When people ask me if I have any spare change, I tell them I have it at home in my spare wallet.

☎ .... **Nick Arnette**

Childhood

When I was a little kid we had a sandbox. It was a quicksand box. I was an only child ... eventually.

☎ .... **Steven Wright**

As I have discovered by examining my past, I started out as a child.

☎ .... **Bill Cosby**

I tell ya when I was a kid, all I knew was rejection. My yo-yo never came back!

☎ ..... **Rodney Dangerfield**

Remember wearing hand-me-downs? I hated that; I have an older sister.

☎ .... **Scott Wood**

There were three kids in my family. One of each sex.

☎ .... **Henny Youngman**

When you're eight years old, nothing is your business.

☎ .... **Lenny Bruce**

We spend the first twelve months of our children's lives teaching them to walk and talk and the next twelve telling them to sit down and shut up.

☎ .... **Phyllis Diller**

I'm nostalgic. I miss child-hood. I miss first grade. I miss thinking girls are gross. Do you know how much money I could save if I still thought girls were gross?

☎ .... **Patrick Keane**

Kids could always resolve any dispute by calling it. One of them will say, "I got the front seat. I called it." And the other kid has no recourse. If there was a kid court of law, it holds up. "Your Honor, my client asked for the front seat." The judge asks, "Did he call it?" "Well, no." He bangs the gavel. "Objection overruled. He has to call it. Case closed."

☎ .... **Jerry Seinfeld**

My kids can be cranky and don't like to take baths. They're like little Europeans.

☎ .... **Brian Kiley**

I'm so ugly, as a kid, I once stuck my head out the window and got arrested for mooning.

☎ ..... **Rodney Dangerfield**

I was the kid next door's imaginary friend.

☎ .... **Emo Philips**

Children

Humans are the only animals that have children on purpose, with the exception of guppies, who like to eat theirs.

☎ .... **P. J. O'Rourke**

Human beings are the only creatures that allow their children to come back home.

☎ .... **Bill Cosby**

Most children threaten at times to run away from home. This is the only thing that keeps some parents going.

☎ .... **Phyllis Diller**

According to an article in *USA Today*, children from single-parent homes have much better verbal skills than children from two-parent homes. However, children from two-parent homes are far superior at bitterly sarcastic repartee.

☎ . . . . **Dennis Miller**

I'm forty-three, and I have a two-year-old. And I did it on purpose, so you know I'm not that bright.

☎ . . . . **Stephanie Hodge**

My wife and I don't have any kids. We don't want any kids, we're happy the way we are. If we have a sudden urge to spank someone, we'll spank each other.

☎ . . . . **Danny Liebert**

I want my children to have all the things I couldn't afford. Then I want to move in with them.

☎ . . . . **Phyllis Diller**

Okay, I admit it. I had a kid so I'd have an excuse to buy Marshmallow Fluff.

☎ . . . . **Caryn Leschen**

Having children gives your life purpose. Right now my purpose is to get some sleep.

☎ . . . . **Reno Goodale**

Cleaning

Cleaning the house before your kids are done growing is like shoveling the walk before it stops snowing.

☎ . . . . **Phyllis Diller**

I'm such a pack rat that when I lost over a hundred pounds, I couldn't throw away my fat clothes. I just bagged them up and put them in the garage, next to my dead husband's clothes. Next to my dead husband.

☎ ... **Johnnye Jones Gibson**

I haven't cleaned up in a while. I've got a messy house, and a milk carton with a picture of the Lindbergh baby on it.

☎ .... **Greg Ray**

Oh, give me a home where the buffalo roam, and I'll show you a house full of dirt.

☎ .... **Marty Allen**

Clichés

I'm tired of all this nonsense about beauty only being skin deep. That's deep enough. What do you want, an adorable pancreas?

☎ .... **Jean Kerr**

Confession is good for the soul only in the sense that a tweed coat is good for dandruff.

☎ .... **Peter De Vries**

I've heard that dogs are man's best friend. That explains where men are getting their hygiene tips.

☎ .... **Kelly Maguire**

Familiarity breeds contempt, and children.

☎ .... **Mark Twain**

Benjamin Franklin said, "Fish and visitors smell in three days," but old friends from college usually smell already.

☎ . . . . P. J. O'Rourke

Did you ever hear someone say this: "It was more fun than a barrel of monkeys"? Did you ever *smell* a barrel of monkeys?

☎ . . . . Steve Bluestein

Laugh, and the world laughs with you. Cry, and the world laughs at you.

☎ . . . . Caryn Leschen

Life's not fair. If it were, my running shoes would keep me running right past all those donut shops.

☎ . . . Johnnye Jones Gibson

Just remember: It's lonely at the top, when there's no one on the bottom.

☎ . . . . . Rodney Dangerfield

It's going to be fun to watch and see how long the meek can keep the earth after they inherit it.

☎ . . . . Kin Hubbard

Money can't buy happiness, but it helps you look for it in more places.

☎ **Milton Berle**

All I ask is the chance to prove that money can't make me happy.

☎ . . . . Spike Milligan

Money really isn't everything. If it were, what would we buy with it?

☎ . . . . **Tom Wilson**

The pen is mightier than the sword, and considerably easier to write with.

☎ . . . . **Marty Feldman**

People say, "A penny saved is a penny earned." Whoever thought up this one must have been saving up for a donut.

☎ . . . . **Pete Zamora**

People who live in glass houses might as well answer the door.

☎ **Morey Amsterdam**

How come it's a penny for your thoughts, but you have to put in your two cents' worth? Somebody's making a penny.

☎ . . . . **Steven Wright**

If at first you don't succeed, failure may be your style.

☎ . . . . **Quentin Crisp**

If at first you don't succeed, stay away from skydiving.

☎ . . . . **Milton Berle**

Time flies like the wind. Fruit flies like a banana.

☎ . . . . **Groucho Marx**

If variety is the spice of life, marriage is the big can of leftover Spam.

☎ . . . . **Johnny Carson**

Clothing

Clothes make the man. Naked people have little or no influence in society.

☎ . . . . **Mark Twain**

The idea behind the tuxedo is the woman's point of view that men are all the same, so we might as well dress that way. That's why a wedding is like the joining together of a beautiful, glowing bride … and some guy. The tuxedo is a wedding safety device. In case the groom chickens out, everybody just takes one step over, and she marries the next guy.

☎ . . . . **Jerry Seinfeld**

The problem with bad jobs is they often make you dress the part. Every time I go to the food court at a mall and see those girls at that lemonade-and-corndog place wearing the red hot-pants and the multicolored hats, I have to bite my tongue to keep from screaming, "Sell your blood!"

☎ . . . . **Dennis Miller**

When a woman tries on clothing from her closet that feels tight, she will assume she has gained weight. When a man tries on clothing from his closet that feels tight, he will assume the clothing has shrunk.

☎ . . . . **Rita Rudner**

Men have an easier time buying bathing suits. Women have two types: depressing, and more depressing. Men have two types: nerdy, and not nerdy.

☎ . . . . **Rita Rudner**

They should put expiration dates on clothing so we men will know when they go out of style.

☎ . . . . **Garry Shandling**

Clowns

In Illinois a clown was arrested for exposing himself. It was the first time anyone ever laughed at him.

☎ . . . . **Jon Stewart**

The hardest part of being a clown, it seems to me, would be that you are constantly referred to as a clown. "Who is that clown?" "I'm not working with that clown." "Did you hire that clown?" "The guy's a clown."

☎ . . . . **Jerry Seinfeld**

Coffee

Studies show that women who drink three cups of coffee or more each day are less likely to commit suicide. Well, yeah, who could hold a gun steady?

☎ . . . . **Margot Black**

I'm on decaf now. What I miss most is the road rage.

☎ . . . . **David Letterman**

There's a new law in West Hollywood: When you buy a cup of coffee, they have to give you a condom. What are they stirring the coffee with? And watch the creamer.

☎ .... **Jay Leno**

I can't handle most stimulants. Anybody else like me? Ya ever call the IHOP at about four in the morning and yell into the phone, "I said *decaf*"?

☎ .... **Tom Ryan**

You can tell a lot about someone's personality by how he orders coffee. "Decaf, please, skim milk, no sugar." That's the kind of a guy who goes through the car wash wearing a seat belt.

☎ .... **Margot Black**

Coffee Houses

There is now a Starbucks in my pants.

☎ .... **George Carlin**

Starbucks celebrated its thirtieth anniversary. And to commemorate the festivities, the aloof chick with the nose ring behind the counter half-smiled.

☎ .... **Bill Maher**

The universe has come to an end in Houston, where there's a Starbucks across the street from a Starbucks. Is this for Alzheimer's sufferers? You finish your coffee and walk out the door and go, "Oh, look, a Starbucks."

☎ .... **Lewis Black**

Did you hear about that guy who's suing Starbucks because he went to the restroom and a defective toilet lid crushed his penis? I thought it was only Denny's that offered the Grand Slam.

☎ .... **David Letterman**

College

Attending college at a place called Bob Jones University is like putting your money in Nick & Tony's Bank.

☎ .... **George Carlin**

I received my degree in calcium anthropology, the study of milkmen.

☎ .... **Steven Wright**

In college I had a triple major: False Advertising, Reverse Psychology, and Broken English.

☎ .... **Tom Ryan**

SAT scores are plummeting, college graduates can't read, and Americans are paying good money for bell-bottoms again. Let's face it, there is an education crisis in this country.

☎ .... **Bill Maher**

One-third of college students in a survey said that they think marijuana should be legalized. The other two-thirds were so paranoid they did not fill out the survey.

☎ .... **Conan O'Brien**

Poor Bush. He can't tell his daughters that if they waste their college years in drinking and partying they'll never amount to anything.

☎ . . . . **Jay Leno**

An eighty-five-year-old woman in Texas just got her university degree. Her parents are delighted. At last she's going to move out of the house.

☎ . . . . **Jay Leno**

Harvard's student body consists of 25 percent Asian Americans. They're afraid that they're going to have to stop admissions based on merit.

☎ . . . . **Al Franken**

Grad school is the snooze button on the clock radio of life.

☎ **John Rogers**

MIT students are going to charm school, learning the etiquette of how to ask what kind of Asian your room-mate is.

☎ . . . . **Jon Stewart**

UCLA decided this week that it is wrong to give preferences based on race. They now say they want college admissions to be based on traditional standards, such as how well you can throw a football, and how much your dad gives to the alumni association.

☎ . . . . **Jay Leno**

I have a master's degree in psychology. I'm over forty, still single, no kids, with a cat, but now I know why.

☎ . . . . **Jill Turnbow**

Cologne

What are men wearing? Why do they think women like horse saddles and pine sap? If a man wanted me to follow him down the street, he should wear something called "Butter Cookie" or, even better, "Croissant."

☎ . . . . **Rita Rudner**

Commercials

Beer commercials usually show big men doing manly things: "You just killed a small animal, it's time for a lite beer." Why not a realistic beer commercial? "It's five o'clock in the morning, you've just pissed in a Dumpster: It's Miller time!"

☎ . . . . **Robin Williams**

They show you how detergents take out blood stains, a pretty violent image. I think if you've got a T-shirt with a bloodstain all over it, maybe laundry isn't your biggest problem. Maybe you should get rid of the body before you do the wash.

☎ . . . . **Jerry Seinfeld**

The Pillsbury Doughboy had his thirtieth birthday last week. A lot of guys get depressed when they turn thirty, and the Doughboy is no different. They found him this morning with his head in the oven.

☎ . . . . **Jay Leno**

Commitment

The Pope is single too. You don't hear people saying he has commitment problems.

☎ . . . . **Garry Shandling**

Why is commitment a big problem for a man? When a man is driving down the freeway of love, the woman he's with is like an exit, but he wants to keep going. The woman says, "Look, gas, food, lodging; everything we need to be happy." But the man is focused on a sign, "Next exit, twenty-seven miles," and thinks, "I can make it." Sometimes he can, sometimes the car ends up on the side of the road, hood up and smoke pouring out of the engine. He's sitting on the curb alone, "I guess I didn't realize how many miles I was racking up."

☎ . . . . **Jerry Seinfeld**

Computers

A computer lets you make more mistakes faster than any invention in human history, with the possible exceptions of handguns and tequila.

☎ . . . . **Mitch Ratliffe**

Computers are invading our whole society. I just saw a tattoo parlor advertising that it has spell check.

☎ . . . . **Jay Leno**

A computer once beat me at chess, but it was no match for me at kick boxing.

☎ . . . . **Emo Philips**

I took a two-year-old computer in to be repaired, and the guy looked at me as though he was a gun dealer, and I'd brought him a musket. In two years I'd gone from cutting edge to Amish.

☎ . . . . **Jon Stewart**

People in the computer industry use the term *user*, which to them means "idiot."

☎ . . . . **Dave Barry**

I don't have a computer. I'm going to wait until that whole fad is over. I was suckered in on the Pet Rock. Not twice, people.

☎ . . . . . . **Kathleen Madigan**

Scientists have invented a computer chip called the nanotubule that is 100,000 times thinner than human hair. It was made by the same machine that slices the roast beef at Arby's.

☎ . . . . **Jay Leno**

Software giant Microsoft was charged with trying to monopolize access to the Internet, and a federal court was asked to fine the company a million dollars per day. Analysts say that at this rate, Microsoft CEO Bill Gates will be broke just ten years after the Earth crashes into the sun.

☎ . . . . **Norm Macdonald**

Bill Gates is only a white Persian cat and a monocle away from being the villain in a James Bond movie.

☎ . . . . **Dennis Miller**

Bill Gates made a pact with the Devil. The Devil said, "You can have $100 billion, but you have to go through life looking like a turtle."

☎ . . . . **Dana Carvey**

Condiments

I've always gotta have a bottle of hot sauce handy, wherever I go. It makes everything taste better. And hey, if I get stuck in an Iowa snowstorm, I could even eat one of my friends.

☎ . . . . **Eric Fleming**

Condoms

There's a new medical crisis. Doctors are reporting that many men are having allergic reactions to latex condoms. They say they cause severe swelling. So what's the problem?

☎ . . . . **Jay Leno**

Conformity

I once complained to my father that I didn't seem to be able to do things the same way other people did. Dad's advice? "Margo, don't be a sheep. People hate sheep. They *eat* sheep."

☎ . . . . **Margo Kaufman**

Congress

If con is the opposite of pro, and progress is good, what is Congress?

☎ . . . . **Gallagher**

You can lead a man to Congress, but you can't make him think.

☎ . . . . **Milton Berle**

Talk is cheap, except when Congress does it.

☎ . . . . **Cullen Hightower**

What Democratic congressmen do to their women staffers, Republican congressmen do to the country.

☎ . . . . **Bill Maher**

Reader, suppose you were an idiot. And suppose you were a member of Congress. But I repeat myself.

☎ . . . . **Mark Twain**

We may not be able to imagine how our lives could be more frustrating and complex, but Congress can.

☎ . . . . **Cullen Hightower**

There are over thirty doctors running for the U.S. Congress this year. That's going to be rather strange. Half the time these folks will be playing God and asking women to take their clothes off and the other half of the time they will be doctors.

☎ . . . . **Jay Leno**

The Senate: Our founding fathers, in their wisdom, devised a method by which our republic can take a hundred of its most prominent numskulls and keep them out of the private sector, where they might do actual harm.

☎ . . . . **P. J. O'Rourke**

The reason there are two senators for each state is so that one can be the designated driver.

☎ . . . . **Jay Leno**

Jesse Helms announced he was retiring after thirty years in office. And Strom Thurmond called him a quitter.

☎ **Bill Maher**

Conspiracies

The biggest conspiracy has always been the fact that there is no conspiracy. Nobody's out to get you. Nobody gives a shit whether you live or die. There, you feel better now?

☎ . . . . **Dennis Miller**

Contraception

Last year was the fortieth anniversary of the most effective birth-control device in history: the TV remote control.

☎ . . . . **Jay Leno**

Other women take the Pill and don't get pregnant. I take the Pill and get a mustache and beard.

☎ . . . . **Andi Rhoads**

Contraceptives should be used on every conceivable occasion.

☎ . . . . **Spike Milligan**

There's a new contraceptive patch for women. It's three inches in diameter and reads, "Get off me."

☎ . . . . **Tina Fey**

Women purchase four out of ten condoms sold. Men wear nine out of ten.

☎ . . . . **Patrick Keane**

Controversy

There are people who can talk sensibly about a controversial issue; they're called humorists.

☎ . . . . **Cullen Hightower**

Cooking

Men are very strange. When they wake up in the morning they want things like toast. I don't have these recipes.

☎ . . . . **Elayne Boosler**

Men like to barbecue. Men will cook if danger is involved.

☎ . . . . **Rita Rudner**

Copiers

I Xeroxed a mirror. Now I have an extra Xerox machine.

☎ . . . . **Steven Wright**

Corporations

So much for corporate patriotism. American Airlines ran a big ad in the newspapers, "Standing with you, the American Airlines family." Then they laid off fifteen thousand employees. I come from a screwed-up family, but when times were tough they didn't can my ass.

☎ . . . . **Norman K.**

Disney will now allow employees to have mustaches. This is part of its program to attract Hungarian women.

☎ . . . . **Craig Kilborn**

The CEO of Firestone has resigned. He's taking a new job with a company that makes children's toys out of plutonium.

☎ . . . . **Jay Leno**

Unilever has bought both Ben & Jerry's and Slim-Fast. They're prepared to make money on any mood swing.

☎ . . . . **Colin Quinn**

Frederick's of Hollywood has gone belly-up. The workers got pink slips with matching panties.

☎ . . . . **Jay Leno**

Philip Morris bought Nabisco. At last, a way to make cigarettes stay crisp in milk.

☎ . . . . **Jon Stewart**

Cosmetics

Sears has announced that it is closing all its cosmetic counters at its retail stores. It turns out that women weren't going for that Sears Weather Beater mascara.

☎ . . . . **Jay Leno**

All men are afraid of eyelash curlers. I sleep with one under my pillow instead of a gun.

☎ . . . . **Rita Rudner**

I don't see the point of testing cosmetics on rabbits, because they're already cute.

☎ . . . . **Rich Hall**

Cosmetic Surgery

My wife asked for plastic surgery; I cut up her credit cards.

☎ ..... **Rodney Dangerfield**

I was going to have cosmetic surgery until I noticed that the doctor's office was full of portraits by Picasso.

☎ .... **Rita Rudner**

Everybody In Los Angeles has cosmetic surgery; I don't know why they bother with a picture ID. When I was growing up a nose job was a very big deal. Now it's like, "Is that your real head?"

☎ .... **Sue Kolinsky**

Drug kingpin Amado Carrillo Fuentes died from nine hours of liposuction and plastic surgery. Or, as it's commonly known here in Beverly Hills, natural causes.

☎ .... **Bill Maher**

Courts

The Supreme Court ruled in favor of the Three Stooges in a dispute involving their image on T-shirts. The court clearly had jurisdiction. Once they decided a United States presidential election, it opened the door for a ruling on the Three Stooges.

☎ .... **Argus Hamilton**

The Supreme Court has outlawed medical marijuana. It's time for me to close my drug clinic in the shoe box under my bed. Marijuana is useful for treating such medical conditions as glaucoma, and visiting dull relatives.

☎ . . . . **Jon Stewart**

Last week a court of appeals in London, England, upheld the British military ban on homosexuals in the service. Kind of ironic, isn't it? Homosexuals being told they can't serve their country by a government guy wearing a robe and a powdered wig.

☎ . . . . **Jay Leno**

Credit Cards

Now my credit cards pay each other. I've stepped out of the picture.

☎ . . . . **Kelly Monteith**

Crime

We live in an age when pizza gets to your home before the police.

☎ . . . . **Jeff Marder**

Police in Concord, California, have arrested two men who robbed a pizza delivery guy after he delivered a pizza to their house. How lazy are people getting in this country when they won't even leave their house to commit a crime?

☎ . . . . **Jay Leno**

In Lowell, Indiana, there was a four-hour hostage standoff in a bank. The bank customers were made to line up and stand still for hours, just like a regular visit.

☎ . . . . **Bill Maher**

I just recently had my Visa card stolen. Right now, it's everywhere I want to be.

☎ **Scott Wood**

I woke up one morning and realized that someone had broken in the night before and replaced everything in my apartment with an exact replica. I got my roommate and showed him. I said, "Look at this, everything's been re-placed with an exact replica!" He said, "Do I know you?"

☎ . . . . **Steven Wright**

We had gay burglars the other night. They broke in and rearranged the furniture.

☎ . . . . **Robin Williams**

The mayor of New York City suspects that the Fulton Fish Market, a longtime New York City landmark, is now being controlled by organized crime. There may be something to that. Today I went there for lunch and I ordered lobster, and they served it tied-up, face-down, in a pool of butter.

☎ . . . . **David Letterman**

Organized crime in America takes in over forty billion dollars a year and spends very little on office supplies.

☎ . . . . **Woody Allen**

Last night about nine P.M., the doorbell rings. A bunch of kids were standing there wearing their gang colors and demanding money. Those Girl Scouts are unbelievable.

☎ . . . . **Paula Bell**

> *They finally got that serial killer. Yup, a Miami jury convicted Joe Camel.*
>
> ☎ **Jay Leno**

The chalk outline of the dead body, how does that help to solve the crime? They look at the thing on the ground, "Oh, his arm was like that when he hit the pavement, the killer must have been . . . Jim!"

☎ . . . . **Jerry Seinfeld**

Robbers who were holding hostages at a Target store were taken into custody and charged with grand theft crap.

☎ . . . . **Craig Kilborn**

A railroad serial killer is out there on the loose. And because he travels by Amtrak, they believe he may also be suicidal.

☎ . . . . **Jay Leno**

In Quebec an eighty-year-old bank robber got one hundred thousand dollars, even though he didn't even have a gun. Evidently, the bank was being guarded by the Sacramento Kings.

☎ . . . . **Craig Kilborn**

I was once arrested for walking in someone else's sleep.

☎ . . . . **Steven Wright**

In West Virginia yesterday, a man was arrested for stealing several blow-up dolls. Reportedly, police didn't have any trouble catching the man because he was completely out of breath.

☎ . . . . **Conan O'Brien**

Authorities raided the home of KKK leader David Duke after accusations that he misused funds earmarked for the white supremacist movement. He bought sheets for his bed instead of his head.

☎ . . . . **Jay Leno**

Charles Manson just turned sixty-seven years old. He's getting very old now. He now has to wear a hearing aid just so he can hear the voices inside his head.

☎ . . . . **Craig Kilborn**

If it wasn't for pickpockets and frisking at airports I'd have no sex life at all.

☎ . . . . . **Rodney Dangerfield**

Culture

There's so much plastic in this culture that vinyl leopard skin is becoming an endangered synthetic.

☎ . . . . **Lily Tomlin**

Dance

I don't like ballet. The last time I went with friends there was a lot of money bet on the swan to live.

☎ . . . . **Woody Allen**

Dating

My friends have been trying to set me up on dates. They mean well, but it's always the same thing. They would say, "We found someone perfect for you." I meet the person and I ask myself, "What do my friends think of me?"

☎ . . . . **Mike Dugan**

I don't want to hang out in bars. If you want to meet people there are basically two ways, and they both suck. Blind dates, which are a disaster. Or getting fixed up, which is just a blind date with witnesses.

☎ . . . . **Robin Roberts**

I think blind dates get a bad rap. They're really not so bad, once you find a restaurant that doesn't mind the dog and has a menu in Braille.

☎ . . . . **Kelly Maguire**

I'm dating a homeless woman. It was easier to talk her into staying over.

☎ . . . . **Garry Shandling**

The men are so rude, especially the lines they come up with. For example, if a man tells you he likes to go for long walks, it means he doesn't own a car. If he says he enjoys romantic dinners at home, it means he's broke.

☎ . . . . **Paula Bell**

I hate when I go to pick up a girl, and she's not ready. I called this girl Keisha at five P.M., said I'd be there at eight P.M. But I get to her place and she's still in her bathrobe. So she must have had sex, and got robbed, before I got there.

☎ . . . . **The Dawk**

Dinner is a waste on a first date, because you don't want the guy to see how much you can really eat. "He'll find out soon enough that I can put my entire head in a Häagen-Dazs tub."

☎ . . . . **Maryellen Hooper**

Guys are so cheap on dates. This guy took me to a coffeehouse for a dollar tea, then starts making moves. I'm like, "Listen buddy, I'm worth more than a cup of tea. You buy me something with foam on it."

☎ . . . . **Maura Kennedy**

I'm kind of lazy. I'm dating a pregnant woman.

☎ **Ron Richards**

This guy I met in a bar said, "When I make love I turn into an animal." Well, that's a step up.

☎ . . . . **Judy Tenuta**

I was dating a stunt man for a while, which is a lot like dating a regular guy. He picks me up, takes me out to dinner, but when he drops me off he doesn't stop the car.

☎ . . . . **Jennifer Siegal**

Single women, date a lot of guys before you get married. I had what I called my series of *Time/Life* boyfriends. I examined them for fourteen days, kept the ones I wanted, and hung on to the free gifts.

☎ . . . . **Traci Skene**

When a man says he wants to meet a girl with a sense of humor, he means one who will laugh at everything he says while her breasts jiggle.

☎ . . . . **Cheri Oteri**

Dating is like driving on the freeway; I can never get to where I'm supposed to be. I know I should be at the corner of "Engaged to Be Married," but instead I'm stuck in the valley of "Haven't Had an Orgasm for Three Months."

☎ . . . . . . **Christine O'Rourke**

What can you do at the end of a date when you know you don't want to see this person ever again, for the rest of your life? What do you say? "I'll see you around." Where is that? "If you're around, and I'm around, I'll see you around that area. You'll be around other people, though. You won't be around me. But you will be around."

☎ . . . . **Jerry Seinfeld**

The only difference between the women I've dated and Charles Manson is that Manson has the decency to look like a nut case when you first meet him.

☎ . . . . **Richard Jeni**

I went to bed with a model. Not bragging or anything; it took me all night to glue it together.

☎ . . . . **Buzz Nutley**

What do I look for in a woman? I look for *me* in a woman.

☎ . . . . **Patrick Keane**

I'm dating a woman now who, evidently, is unaware of it.

☎ . . . . **Garry Shandling**

I can't even tell if women like me. I know when they don't like me, because they say things like, "Yeah, that's him, Officer."

☎ . . . . **Kevin Brennan**

We men are driven to meet Miss Right, or at least Miss Right Now.

☎ . . . . **Robin Williams**

When I eventually met Mr. Right I had no idea that his first name was Always.

☎ . . . . **Rita Rudner**

My grandmother's ninety. She's dating. He's ninety-three. They're very happy; they never argue. They can't hear each other.

☎ . . . . **Cathy Ladman**

Death

Death is one of the few things that can be done as easily lying down.

☎ . . . . **Woody Allen**

Last month, my aunt passed away. She was cremated. We think that's what did it.

☎ . . . . **Jonathan Katz**

When I die, I want to go peacefully like my grandfather did, in his sleep. Not screaming, like the passengers in his car.

☎ . . . . **Michael Jeffreys**

I want to die with a smile on my face. Hopefully, it won't be mine.

☎ . . . . **Matt Vance**

My cousin just died. He was only nineteen. He got stung by a bee, the natural enemy of a tightrope walker.

☎ . . . . **Emo Philips**

Death is just nature's way of telling you to slow down.

☎ . . . . **Dick Sharples**

Officials are investigating the deaths of men who had taken Viagra. Here's a scary thought: What if Viagra doesn't cure impotence? What if it's just early signs of rigor mortis?

☎ . . . . **Jay Leno**

There are worse things in life than death. Have you ever spent an evening with an insurance salesman?

☎ . . . . **Woody Allen**

Death Penalty

Capital punishment turns the state into a murderer. But imprisonment turns the state into a gay dungeon-master.

☎ . . . . Emo Philips

Backers of the reinstatement of the death penalty in New York claim that it'll make criminals think twice before shooting someone. I don't believe that. When New Yorkers think twice about shooting someone, it means they'll shoot them twice.

☎ . . . . Jay Leno

You know the good part about all those executions in Texas? Fewer Texans.

☎ . . . . George Carlin

A death row inmate in Texas is in trouble for selling tickets on eBay to his own execution. But what can they do to him? Death plus six months?

☎ . . . . Jay Leno

Décor

Martha Stewart is going to show you how you can take things you find dead on the highway and turn your home into a showplace.

☎ . . . . David Letterman

I don't need a reading lamp in my living room. I don't have a toilet in there.

☎ . . . . Norm Macdonald

In my house, on the ceilings I have paintings of the rooms above, so I never have to go upstairs.

☎ . . . . **Steven Wright**

Dentists

My dental hygienist is cute. Every time I visit, I eat a whole package of Oreo cookies while waiting in the lobby. Sometimes she has to cancel the rest of the afternoon appointments.

☎ . . . . **Steven Wright**

Barry Manilow is recovering from an infection after dental surgery. When asked about it, Manilow said, "The worst part was having to sit in the dentist's chair and listen to my crappy music."

☎ . . . . **Conan O'Brien**

Dictionaries

If a word in the dictionary was misspelled, how would we know?

☎ . . . . **Steven Wright**

Diets

I lost twenty pounds. Unfortunately, I was in England at the time.

☎ . . . . **Daniel Lybra**

Dr. Atkins, who promotes the fat and meat diet, is at odds with Dr. Ornish, who believes in whole grains and veggies. They had a big fight at a nutrition conference, and Atkins won: He ate Ornish.

☎ . . . . **Danny Liebert**

You know it's time to go on a diet when you're standing next to your car and get a ticket for double parking.

☎ . . . . **Totie Fields**

I hate dieting, but I've gotta do it. Last week I read about a diet that says, "Just eat half of everything you like," and I'm doing it diligently. Today I've eaten half a stick of celery, and half a pig.

☎ . . . . **Sally Jackson**

I'm trying a new diet now: Viagra and prune juice. I tell ya, I don't know if I'm coming or going.

☎ . . . . . **Rodney Dangerfield**

Differently Abled

If blind people wear sunglasses, why don't deaf people wear earmuffs?

☎ . . . . **Spanky**

A blind man is attempting to climb Mount Everest. Why? "Because somebody told me it was there."

☎ . . . . **Craig Kilborn**

I saw a man with a wooden leg, and a real foot.

☎ . . . . **Steven Wright**

You know the hardest thing about having cerebral palsy and being a woman? It's plucking your eyebrows. That's how I originally got pierced ears.

☎ . . . . **Geri Jewell**

Authorities confiscated the artificial leg of a prisoner who took it off and used it as a weapon in a fight. Was he hitting the other guy or kicking him? In any event, the prisoner is hopping mad.

☎ . . . . **Jay Leno**

A South Korean man with no hands failed in his attempt to climb Mount Everest. He blamed the failure on his lack of hands, the fact that he has no hands, and his handless arms.

☎ . . . . **Craig Kilborn**

Discipline

What am I supposed to do when a teenager points a gun in my face, tell him it's time for a time-out?

☎ . . . . **Sinbad**

Disease

Because of the foot-and-mouth disease, the United States is cracking down on tainted beef from Europe. And as a result, the U.S. is deporting Fabio.

☎ . . . . **Conan O'Brien**

What's the problem? Hooves and mouths are the worst parts of the cow, so why don't we just eat around them?

☎ . . . . **Andy Kindler**

Those cows are saying, "You're eating us, drinking us, wearing us, and sneaking up on us and tipping us over. That's why we're mad."

☎ . . . . **Jerry Seinfeld**

Divorce

You know your marriage is in trouble when your wife starts wearing the wedding ring on her middle finger.

☎ . . . . **Dennis Miller**

I'm not upset about my divorce. I'm only upset I'm not a widow.

☎ . . . . **Roseanne**

Ah, yes, divorce, from the Latin word meaning to rip out a man's genitals through his wallet.

☎ . . . . **Robin Williams**

My first wife divorced me because I didn't match her shoes. I was a lazy white loafer.

☎ . . . . **Kelly Monteith**

My wife left me for my best friend. Now I don't have a dog.

☎ . . . . . **Rodney Dangerfield**

It wasn't actually a divorce. I was traded.

☎ . . . . **Tim Conway**

My wife and I got remarried. Our divorce didn't work out.

☎ . . . . **Henny Youngman**

Marrying a divorced man is ecologically responsible. In a world where there are more women than men, it pays to recycle.

☎ .... **Rita Rudner**

Ever watch one of those Lifetime specials about divorce? They always seem so tragic; they bear no resemblance to my life. "She had it all: husband, children, non-threatening hair. She lost it all!" I'm like, "Can we fast-forward to the part where she marries the pool boy?"

☎ .... **Maura Kennedy**

Think if Mrs. Satan ever wanted to take Satan to the cleaners. Can you imagine how many divorce lawyers there are in hell?

☎ .... **Craig Kilborn**

Doctors

The *New England Journal of Medicine* reports that nine out of ten doctors agree: one out of ten doctors is an idiot.

☎ .... **Jay Leno**

A New York doctor is in a lot of trouble for allegedly operating on the wrong side of his patient's brain. In his defense, the doctor said, "Hey, it's not my fault. Someone once operated on the wrong side of my brain."

☎ .... **Conan O'Brien**

Dr. Kevorkian, the suicide doctor, has applied for a concealed-weapon permit. He wants to carry a gun now. In fact, when he applied, he told the clerk: "Hey, guns don't kill people, I kill people."

☎ .... **Jay Leno**

In North Dakota, doctors removed a man's testicles only to find out later that the procedure wasn't necessary. The man thought about suing but decided not to because he doesn't have the balls.

☎ .... **Conan O'Brien**

Doctors are the only people that if they don't find anything wrong they still charge you. You know what you should do? Next time look into your wallet and say you can't find anything either.

☎ .... **Mark Schiff**

Dogs

Chihuahua, there's a waste of dog food. Looks like a dog that is still far away.

☎ .... **Billiam Coronel**

I've got a Chihuahua. They're good. If you lose one, just empty out your purse.

☎ .... **Jean Carroll**

I wonder if other dogs think poodles are members of a weird religious cult.

☎ .... **Rita Rudner**

I bought a dog the other day. I named him Stay. It's fun to call him, "Come here, Stay! Come here, Stay!" He went insane. Now he just ignores me and keeps typing.

☎ .... **Steven Wright**

They say a dog is man's best friend, but I don't buy it. How many of your friends have had you neutered?

☎ .... **Larry Reeb**

The other day I was walking my dog around my building, on the ledge.

☎ **Steven Wright**

Did you ever walk in a room and forget why you walked in? I think that's how dogs spend their lives.

☎ .... **Sue Murphy**

On my block a lot of people walk their dogs, and I always see them walking along with their little poop bags. This, to me, is the lowest activity in human life. If aliens are watching this through telescopes, they're going to think the dogs are the leaders of the planet. If you see two life forms, one of them is making a poop, the other one's carrying it for him, who would you assume is in charge?

☎ .... **Jerry Seinfeld**

I put contact lenses in my dog's eyes. They had little pictures of cats on them. Then I took one out and he ran around in circles.

☎ . . . . **Steven Wright**

If you pick up a starving dog and make him prosperous, he will not bite you. This is the principal difference between a man and a dog.

☎ . . . . **Mark Twain**

Donation

In a poll, one in four said they'd donate a kidney to a complete stranger. Right, while 90 percent won't let a stranger merge in traffic.

☎ . . . . **Jay Leno**

Drinking

Scientists have located the gene that causes alcoholism. They found it at a party talking too loudly.

☎ . . . . **Conan O'Brien**

Every alcoholic who has stopped drinking can re-member the last time he got drunk. For me, it was the night I drank so much Crown Royal my scrotum turned into a purple pouch with a gold-tasseled drawstring.

☎ . . . . **Jeff Shaw**

A study found teenage girls who drink are much more sexually active. The study was funded by teenage boys.

☎ . . . . **Jay Leno**

I drink too much. Last time I gave a urine sample there was an olive in it.

☎ ..... **Rodney Dangerfield**

A bar in New York is installing a Breathalyzer. If you're drunk, it advises you not to drive. If you're very, very drunk, it advises you not to call your old girlfriend.

☎ .... **Conan O'Brien**

Do you know how old you have to be to drink alcohol in Texas? Neither do the Bush twins.

☎ **Jay Leno**

Driving

The one thing that unites all human beings, regardless of age, gender, religion, economic status, or ethnic background, is that, deep down inside, we all believe that we are above-average drivers.

☎ .... **Dave Barry**

Who are safer drivers? Men, or women? Well, according to a new survey, 55 percent of adults feel women are most responsible for minor fender-benders, while 78 percent blame men for most fatal crashes. Please note that the percentages do not add up to 100 percent, because the math was done by a woman.

☎ .... **Norm Macdonald**

About 7 percent of California drivers say they read a book while driving. Californians reading?

☎ .... **Jay Leno**

One of the first things they teach you in Driver's Ed is where to put your hands on the steering wheel—at ten o'clock and two o'clock. I put mine at 9:45 and 2:17. Gives me an extra half-hour to get where I'm goin'.

☎ .... **George Carlin**

In Toronto, a teenager was taking her driving test and crashed into six cars while trying to parallel park. She won't be able to drive in Canada, but on the bright side, she was issued a New York taxi license.

☎ .... **Conan O'Brien**

Today I can't drive without my daughter in a special car seat, strapped in. We sent John Glenn into space with a Jethro Bodine seat belt.

☎ .... **Jeff Foxworthy**

I hate traffic because I always get stuck behind an old person when I'm driving. All I can see is two hands on the steering wheel. When I see a big hat I know it's an old man; a small hat is an old lady.

☎ .... **Irit Noy**

Signs on the freeway are funny. "Orange Cones Mean Men at Work." What else could orange cones mean? Psychedelic witches embedded in asphalt?

☎ .... **Karin Babbitt**

Traffic signals in New York are just rough guidelines.

☎ .... **David Letterman**

Everything is drive-through. In California they even have burial service called Jump-in-the-Box.

☎ .... **Wil Shriner**

A man in Sacramento kept going to the Department of Motor Vehicles in disguise and got eighty-three drivers' licenses. He spent 95 percent of his life standing in line.

☎ .... **Jay Leno**

I was stopped once for doing fifty-three in a thirty-five-mile-per-hour zone, but I got off. I told them I had dyslexia.

☎ .... **Spanky**

I was pulled over for speeding today. The officer said, "Don't you know the speed limit is fifty-five miles an hour?" I replied, "Yes, but I wasn't going to be out that long."

☎ .... **Steven Wright**

I think it would be fun if people used their age as the speed limit. Old people going eighty to ninety miles per hour, and they'd be that much closer to death.

☎ .... **Irit Noy**

If you think about it, a clown, if there isn't a circus around them, is really just a very annoying person. I mean, you're in the back seat of this guy's Volkswagen. "What, you're picking more people up? Oh, man!"

☎ .... **Jerry Seinfeld**

I was driving down the highway, and I'm swerving all over, 'cuz I'm trying to change the radio, and just as I get the old one taken out I hear this traffic cop behind me, "*Whee-oo, whee-oo, whee-oo!*" Well, I shouldn't make fun of his speech impediment.

☎ . . . . **Emo Philips**

I had to stop driving my car for a while. The tires got dizzy.

☎ . . . . **Steven Wright**

Zooming gas prices have everyone stunned. According to a survey, if gas goes up to twenty, thirty dollars a gallon, people in L.A. may seriously start thinking about walking the two blocks to the store.

☎ . . . . **Jay Leno**

Basically, my husband has two beliefs in life. He believes in God, and he believes that when the gas gauge is on empty, he still has a quarter of a tank. He thinks that "E" stands for "Eeegghh, there's still some left."

☎ . . . . **Rita Rudner**

Drugs

Cocaine, what a wonderful drug. Anything that makes you paranoid and impotent, give me more of that!

☎ . . . . **Robin Williams**

Now they're calling drugs an epidemic: That's 'cause white folks are doing it.

☎ . . . . **Richard Pryor**

Customs agents found five pounds of cocaine in cans of dog food. How dumb is that? If the drug-sniffing dogs don't detect the cocaine, they'll still go for the dog food.

☎ .... **Jay Leno**

I would never do crack. I would never do a drug named after a part of my own ass, okay?

☎ .... **Denis Leary**

No drug, not even alcohol, causes the fundamental ills of society. If we're looking for the source of our troubles, we shouldn't test people for drugs; we should test them for stupidity, ignorance, greed, and love of power.

☎ .... **P. J. O'Rourke**

In Florida a seventy-two-year-old woman was arrested for having several bags of marijuana in her possession. Police became suspicious of the woman after she knit a bong.

☎ .... **Craig Kilborn**

A small town in the Netherlands is planning to open several drive-through restaurants that will sell marijuana. Here's how it works: At the first window you order the pot; at the second window you smoke the pot; and at the third window you order fifty-seven cheeseburgers.

☎ .... **Conan O'Brien**

The Supreme Court has out-lawed medical marijuana. Many users were so upset they almost got up off the couch. Sales of medical Cheetos have plummeted.

☎ . . . . **Jay Leno**

Switzerland is legalizing marijuana. They make the most accurate clocks in the world, and no one will care what time it is. And how much chocolate are they going to sell now?

☎ . . . . **Conan O'Brien**

Medicinal marijuana? Can't we start slower? Medicinal chocolate? Medicinal whiskey?

☎ . . . . **Patrick Keane**

Several states have a mari-juana initiative. The Marijuana Initiative. I like saying it. It's the only time you get to say *marijuana* and *initiative* in the same sentence.

☎ . . . . **Jay Leno**

Scientists have shown mon-keys can become addicted to marijuana. Another group that can become addicted? Scientists. Of course, the monkeys all had glaucoma.

☎ . . . . **Jon Stewart**

The best mind-altering drug is truth.

☎ **Lily Tomlin**

FedEx employees shipped 121 tons of marijuana. When it absolutely, positively has to be there whenever.

☎ .... **Jay Leno**

George W. Bush submitted to a urine test. But beforehand he wrote the answers on his hand.

☎ .... **Conan O'Brien**

Dry Cleaners

A good place to meet a man is at the dry cleaner. These men usually have jobs and bathe.

☎ .... **Rita Rudner**

Earthquakes

My family and I have come up with a course of action for an earthquake. At the first tremor, we get out of bed calmly, stand in a doorway, and start screaming. Maybe you know our system under another name: panic.

☎ .... **Milton Berle**

There was a big earthquake in Seattle, registering 6.8 on the Richter scale. No one was seriously hurt, but a lot of buildings collapsed. On one block alone more than four hundred Starbucks were destroyed.

☎ .... **Conan O'Brien**

Economical

When I heated my home with oil, I used an average of eight hundred gallons a year. I have found that I can keep comfortably warm for an entire winter with slightly over half that quantity of beer.

☎ .... Dave Barry

Economists

An economist is an expert who will know tomorrow why the things he predicted yesterday didn't happen today.

☎ .... Evan Esar

Economists predict that this year's federal surplus will be $120 billion less than predicted in January. The missing $120 billion was reportedly last seen on a date with Congressman Gary Condit.

☎ .... Dennis Miller

Economy

You want to see an economically sound, well-run country, privatize the whole shooting match. Why not the Coca-Cola White House or the Home Depot Supreme Court? It's not like we already don't have the Smith & Wesson House of Representatives and the Philip Morris Senate.

☎ .... Dennis Miller

When the high-tech economy tanks, the Amish will take over. They've got us by the udders, and we never saw it coming.

☎ .... **Dave Attell**

Education

You know there is a problem with the education system when you realize that out of the three Rs, only one begins with a R.

☎ .... **Dennis Miller**

Reading, which gave us Shakespeare and Dostoevsky, is being replaced by a visual culture that has made me so sick of seeing Madonna naked that I might as well be married to her.

☎ .... **Bill Maher**

I took a course in speed-reading and was able to read *War and Peace* in twenty minutes. It's about Russia.

☎ .... **Woody Allen**

Sex education will encourage kids to have sex? No way. I had four years of algebra and I never do math.

☎ .... **Elayne Boosler**

They say Japanese teenagers are smarter than American teens. Oh yeah? Let's see a Japanese kid earn a diploma without knowing how to read.

☎ .... **Jeff Shaw**

President Bush signed an education bill with Teddy Kennedy. They're both living examples of the importance of education. Thanks to years of study, they learned that the best way to get elected president is to quit drinking at forty.

☎ .... **Argus Hamilton**

The world's largest oil rig exploded and sank off Brazil. The company said the environmental impact would be minimal, partly because of the isolated location, and partly because they're lying through their teeth.

☎ .... **Jon Stewart**

Environment

There's so much pollution in the air now that if it weren't for our lungs, there'd be no place to put it all.

☎ .... **Robert Orben**

There was an embarrassing moment during George W. Bush's environmental speech in the Everglades. A bunch of Al Gore ballots floated by.

☎ .... **David Letterman**

It's hard for me to get used to these changing times. I can remember when the air was clean and sex was dirty.

☎ .... **George Burns**

Those topless women protesting clear-cutting of the forests have come up with an effective approach: "Save the trees. Take a look at these."

☎ .... **Jay Leno**

Dick Cheney wants more nuclear power, drilling for oil, and use of coal. He says nuclear plants emit no carbon dioxide. So our grandchildren can breathe clean air safely through their gills.

☎ . . . . **Jon Stewart**

Australians have been knitting sweaters to protect penguins from an oil spill. The penguins say they'd rather die than dress informal.

☎ . . . . **Conan O'Brien**

There was a runaway train with toxic chemicals in Ohio. It was moving forward, endangering the environment, with no one in charge. Just like the Bush administration.

☎ . . . . **Jay Leno**

Ethnicity

I heard about an Amish guy getting run over by a car. That's like a Catholic choking on a condom.

☎ . . . . **Renee Hicks**

I'm from a mixed background. My mother is Asian and my dad is Mexican. So don't blame me if I'm a bad driver without insurance.

☎ . . . . **Pete Zamora**

Some people say all black people look alike. We call those people "police."

☎ . . . . **Dave Chappelle**

In a speech today George W. Bush made up a whole new word:"Hispanically," meaning "not Caucasian-able."

☎ . . . . **Conan O'Brien**

I'm Irish and Dutch. Which means my idea of a good time is to get drunk and drive my car into a windmill.

☎ . . . . **Kris McGaha**

I'm Italian, but my friends are like, "Oh, my God, you look Jewish." This is good; I'm leaving work early for the holidays. "Hi, my name is Tracy Esposito . . . witz. Gotta go, the sun's comin' down. Happy Rosha Hannukah."

☎ . . . . **Tracy Esposito**

I'm half Italian and half Polish. So I'm always putting a hit out on myself.

☎ . . . . **Judy Tenuta**

Euthanasia

If I'm ever stuck on a respirator or a life support system I definitely want to be unplugged. But not until I'm down to a size eight.

☎ . . . . **Henriette Mantel**

Dr. Kevorkian was granted an emergency permit to carry a handgun, after telling a court he fears "right-wing nuts." But if you ask me, I think he's just getting a little lazy.

☎ . . . . **Norm Macdonald**

Evolution

My theory of evolution is that Darwin was adopted.

☎ .... **Steven Wright**

If evolution was worth its salt, it should've evolved something better than "survival of the fittest." I think a better idea would be "survival of the wittiest." At least that way, creatures that didn't survive could've died laughing.

☎ .... **Lily Tomlin**

Exercise

I don't exercise. What's in it for me? You've got to offer me more than my life to get me on a Stairmaster grunting for two hours. I view my body as a way of getting my head from one place to the other.

☎ .... **Dave Thomas**

It takes six months to get into shape and two weeks to get out of shape. Once you know this you can stop being angry about other things in life and only be angry about this.

☎ .... **Rita Rudner**

Oh yeah, I'll continue to work out—until I get married.

☎ .... **Tom Arnold**

I get plenty of exercise carrying the coffins of my friends who exercise.

☎ . . . . **Red Skelton**

If it weren't for the fact that the TV set and the refrigerator are so far apart, some of us wouldn't get any exercise at all.

☎ . . . . **Joey Adams**

My boyfriend is a fitness trainer, very enthusiastic. He loves doing bench presses and squats. I have my favorite exercises, too: the refrigerator lunge, followed by the microwave push.

☎ . . . . **Andi Rhoads**

The word *aerobics* came about when the gym instructors got together and said, "If we're going to charge ten dollars an hour, we can't call it Jumping Up and Down."

☎ . . . . **Rita Rudner**

As a nation we are dedicated to keeping physically fit, and parking as close to the stadium as possible.

☎ **Bill Vaughan**

I thought Spinning was this exotic new exercise at the gym, but it's just a bunch of people riding stationary bicycles. Yeah, and they're renaming the Stairmaster, "Stomping."

☎ . . . . **Denise Robb**

Eyesight

I went to the eye doctor and found out I needed glasses for reading. So I got flip-up contact lenses.

☎ . . . . **Steven Wright**

I had a lazy eye as a kid, and it gradually spread to my whole body.

☎ . . . . **Tom Cotter**

I have such poor vision, I can date anybody.

☎ . . . . **Garry Shandling**

Family

I grew up in a big family, six kids. Seven, if you count my dad. Man, he got all the attention, being the youngest.

☎ . . . . **Margaret Smith**

When I was four, my mom forgot me on the sidewalk once, by accident. At least I like to believe it was an accident, because when the police officer brought me back home, my family had moved!

☎ . . . . **Cecile Lubrani**

Fashion

Never let a panty line show around your ankle.

☎ . . . . **Joan Rivers**

When I was a boy my mother wore a mood ring. When she was in a good mood, it turned blue. In a bad mood, it left a big red mark on my forehead.

☎ .... **Jeff Shaw**

I ate at McDonald's and I got sick. My reflection in the mirror looked pale and my lips turned red. Then I realized where they got the idea for the clown.

☎ .... **Pete Zamora**

Fast Food

I started a grease fire at McDonald's. Threw a match in the cook's hair.

☎ .... **Steve Martin**

McDonalds is going to sell deli food. Right now they're training sixteen-year-old illegal aliens to make chopped liver. You'll be able to have scalding hot matzo ball soup dumped in your lap.

☎ .... **David Letterman**

I went into a McDonald's yesterday and said, "I'd like some fries." The girl at the counter asked, "Would you like some fries with that?"

☎ .... **Jay Leno**

A Virginia woman found a chicken head in her McNuggets. At first she thought it was a Mick Jagger action figure. Actually, it's just McDonald's new voodoo meal.

☎ .... **Jay Leno**

A handwritten note was found in a home once owned by Kentucky Fried Chicken founder Colonel Sanders. And for several days, it was thought to contain the Colonel's secret recipe. Eventually, they realized the recipe was fake because it requires using "real chicken."

☎ . . . . **Conan O'Brien**

Fathers

If the new American father feels bewildered and even defeated, let him take comfort from the fact that whatever he does in any fathering situation has a 50 percent chance of being right.

☎ . . . . **Bill Cosby**

I was raised by just my mom. See, my father died when I was eight years old. At least, that's what he told us in the letter.

☎ . . . . **Drew Carey**

I never know what to get my father for his birthday. I gave him one hundred dollars and said, "Buy yourself something that will make your life easier." So he bought a present for my mother.

☎ . . . . **Rita Rudner**

Fatherhood is pretending the present you love most is soap-on-a-rope.

☎ . . . . **Bill Cosby**

I have mixed emotions when I receive my Father's Day gifts. I'm glad my children remember me; I'm disappointed that they actually think I dress like that.

☎ . . . . **Mike Dugan**

Tony Randall, seventy-eight, became a father again. Tony says he just wants to live long enough to see his kids graduate preschool.

☎ . . . . **Jay Leno**

Faxes

For Christmas I bought my brother a combination fax machine and paper shredder. Either we hooked it up wrong or a lot of people are faxing him confetti.

☎ . . . . **Anthony Clark**

I got a chain letter by fax. It's very simple. You just fax a dollar bill to everybody on the list.

☎ . . . . **Steven Wright**

Feminism

I don't call myself a feminist. I call myself a killer bitch.

☎ . . . . **Roseanne**

Fire

Isn't it odd that when a house burns down, the only things left standing are the chimney and the fireplace?

☎ . . . . **Steven Wright**

They're using water-dropping planes to put out the fires around L.A. Doors in the belly open, and water falls out. It's the same technique Southwest uses with luggage.

☎ . . . . **Jay Leno**

Fireplaces

I have a microwave fireplace in my house. The other night I laid down in front of the fire for the evening in two minutes.

☎ . . . . **Steven Wright**

Flowers

Flowers are one of the few things we buy, bring home, watch die, and we don't ask for our money back.

☎ . . . . **George Carlin**

Flying

Airports have a curious smell that is a delicate mixture of jet exhaust, bad food, spilled beer, and hundreds of thousands of armpits emitting numerous levels of toxicity according to various cultural hygienic mores. Try to picture an international rainbow of stink.

☎ . . . . **Dennis Miller**

Getting on a plane, I told the ticket lady, "Send one of my bags to New York, send one to Los Angeles, and send one to Miami." She said, "We can't do that." I told her, "You did it last week."

☎ . . . . **Henny Youngman**

They have luggage stores in airports. Who forgets their suitcase? Have you ever seen a guy with an armload of shirts going, "Hurrah, a suitcase!"

☎ . . . . **Jay Mohr**

When they closed Denver's old Stapleton Airport, the gift shop had a big clearance sale, everything 90 percent off. This was great: You could get a bottle of aspirin for twenty dollars.

☎ . . . . **Jay Leno**

There's a lot of terrorism in the air, but when you walk through the air terminal and see the crack security people manning the perimeter, I think we all sleep the sleep of angels. Came into Phoenix the other day, the woman working the X-ray machine had the attention span of Boo Radley. She's sitting there like Captain Pike from *Star Trek*. She had a channel flicker. She's watching baggage from other airports, for Christ's sake.

☎ . . . . **Dennis Miller**

They've unveiled a new security plan for aviation today. Every plane will now have a hockey dad on board.

☎ **David Letterman**

Are there keys to a plane? Maybe that's what those delays are. They tell you it's mechanical because they don't want to come on the P.A. system, "Ladies and gentlemen, we're going to be on the ground for a while. I, uh, I left the keys to the plane in my apartment. They're in this big ashtray by the front door. I'm sorry, I'll run back and get them."

☎ . . . . **Jerry Seinfeld**

A lot of qualifications to sit next to that exit door, huh? I've been a physical klutz for years. I'm like Clouseau, all of a sudden they want me to be a Navy SEAL. I guess they want to be sure the person sitting there doesn't panic in the event that the plane goes down in water. Item number 8 on the qualification list was "You must not be Ted Kennedy."

☎ . . . . **Dennis Miller**

Never play peekaboo with a child on a long plane trip. There's no end to the game. Finally I grabbed him by the bib and said, "Look, it's *always* gonna be me!"

☎ . . . . **Rita Rudner**

A lady is suing Continental Airlines because she had to sit next to a dead guy. The guy was definitely dead, colder than a TWA dinner roll.

☎ . . . . **David Letterman**

Am I the only one who likes to get on a plane and sit there in a little peace and quiet? I'm constantly in conversation with complete strangers, always being approached by these overly ebullient Jonathan Livingston Human types. He's got a dream he wants me to interpret for him. And you're afraid to not talk to him; you never know if a terrorist is on the plane. I'd hate to alienate anybody who's looking for a prom date to Valhalla.

☎ . . . . **Dennis Miller**

I love the sign in the airplane bathroom, "As a courtesy to the next passenger, please wipe off the counter with towel." Sorry, I forgot to bring my toilet brush with me. When did this Brotherhood of Passengers get started? "Did they lose your luggage? Here, take mine. By the way, was the bathroom clean enough for you? I couldn't find the Comet or I would've had that crapper gleaming."

☎ . . . . **Jerry Seinfeld**

The National Council on Psychic Research has officially designated this to be true: The experience of changing planes in New York now counts as a near-death experience.

☎ . . . . **David Letterman**

A couple got married on a Continental Airlines flight last week. They had the whole service on the plane. That's kind of odd, don't you think? All your life you dream about walking down the aisle, the big moment comes and you're stuck behind the beverage cart.

☎ .... **Jay Leno**

A passenger aboard Olympic Airlines was arrested after he stripped naked aboard the airplane. The passenger claims he misunderstood the stewardess when she asked if he wanted salted nuts.

☎ .... **Conan O'Brien**

Food

There's a new 'N Sync candy. It hangs out with the Britney Spears candy bar but never gets inside her wrapper.

☎ .... **Conan O'Brien**

I like any cereal. I like the idea of just eating and drinking with one hand, without looking.

☎ .... **Jerry Seinfeld**

Little kids in a supermarket buy cereal the way men buy lingerie. They get stuff they have no interest in just to get the prize inside.

☎ .... **Jeff Foxworthy**

The Department of Agriculture says that two pellets of rat fecal matter is now acceptable in every two kilograms of breakfast cereal. Actually, do you know what the technical name for grain and fecal matter in food is? A hot dog.

☎ .... **Jay Leno**

The Heinz Corporation has just come out with a new chocolate French fry. A French fry that is chocolate. Sounds like the white trash Valentine's Day gift.

☎ .... **Jay Leno**

> *Red meat is not bad for you. Now, blue-green meat,* that's *bad for you.*
>
> ☎ **Tommy Smothers**

I just gave up dairy, caffeine, and sugar because I was feeling sluggish, tired, and anxious. Now I have a lot more energy to feel angry and deprived.

☎ .... **Jennifer Siegal**

Chinese-German food is wonderful. The only problem is, an hour later you're hungry for power.

☎ .... **Dick Cavett**

Scientists are now saying eating meat is as bad for you as smoking. And if you eat smoked meat ... But what you really have to watch out for is secondhand meat.

☎ .... **Jay Leno**

As a child my family's menu consisted of two choices: Take it, or leave it.

☎ .... **Buddy Hackett**

McDonald's is coming out with a new mega-burger: four patties, 790 calories, 41 grams of fat. Now McDonald's has a complete menu: the Breakfast Meal, the Happy Meal, and the Last Meal.

☎ **Jay Leno**

If a man prepares dinner for you and the salad contains three or more types of lettuce, he is serious.

☎ .... **Rita Rudner**

I was in a supermarket and I saw Paul Newman's face on salad dressing and spaghetti sauce. I thought he was missing.

☎ .... **Bob Saget**

A new product out now, Diet Coke with lemon. Didn't that used to be called Pledge?

☎ .... **Jay Leno**

I used to think I was poor, but I'm moving up in the world. Three weeks ago, I bought my first *case* of spicy chicken ramen noodles. The expensive kind that comes in a cup.

☎ .... **Eric Fleming**

General Mills is coming out with an organic Twinkie. Isn't that called a sponge?

☎ .... **Jay Leno**

Eating tofu can reduce your chances of catching certain diseases. Most people would rather catch the diseases.

☎ . . . . **Craig Kilborn**

Ben and Jerry are breaking up over the failure of their new ice cream flavor, Strawberry Rehab.

☎ . . . . **David Letterman**

A few years ago, the tobacco industry considered developing a tobacco-based lollipop. If that weren't bad enough, when you bit through the lollipop, there was a chewy heroin center.

☎ . . . . **Conan O'Brien**

Purdue University researchers now say that eating a lot of hamburgers can prevent skin cancer. That's good, because if you eat a lot of hamburgers, you might have a lot of extra skin to protect.

☎ . . . . **Jay Leno**

Football

Football combines the two worst features of American life: violence and committee meetings.

☎ . . . . **George Will**

In the NFL these days when they tackle a player they have to hold him down until the police arrive. Court TV has been named the official network of the NFL.

☎ . . . . **Jay Leno**

The NFL Experience theme park opened down in New Orleans. It's really something; you get to feel what it's like to be a pro. They give you a football, then some cocaine and take your mug shot. So you get the whole experience!

☎ . . . . **Jay Leno**

Coaching salaries have reached astronomical levels. Bill Gates spent yesterday morning diagramming foot-ball plays until his hands bled.

☎ . . . . **Argus Hamilton**

A poll shows women think men are sexiest playing football. And they're at their least sexy watching football.

☎ . . . . **Jay Leno**

The NFL players association has agreed to a brand-new contract that would run through the year 2007. Meanwhile, the XFL players association has agreed to work the late shift at 7-Eleven.

☎ . . . . **Conan O'Brien**

Dennis Miller joined *Monday Night Football.* Viewers enjoy watching the game while flipping through a dictionary and a thesaurus.

☎ . . . . **Craig Kilborn**

More news on that Notre Dame football coach. George O'Leary, the guy that lied about his résumé, has found a new job as an assistant with the Vikings. It was that or back to his old job of taking care of financial reports for Enron.

☎ . . . . **Jay Leno**

Foreign Language

I bought one of those tapes to teach you Spanish in your sleep. During the night, the tape skipped. Now I can only stutter in Spanish.

☎ . . . . **Steven Wright**

I saw a close friend of mine the other day. He said, "How come you haven't called me?" I said, "I can't call everyone I want. My new phone has no 5 on it." He said, "How long have you had it?" I said, "I don't know, my calendar has no 7s."

☎ . . . . **Steven Wright**

Friends

One good reason to maintain only a small circle of friends is that three out of four murders are committed by people who know the victim.

☎ . . . . **George Carlin**

An old friend will help you move. A good friend will help you move a dead body.

☎ . . . . **Jim Hayes**

Funerals

I didn't attend the funeral, but I sent a nice letter saying I approved of it.

☎ . . . . **Mark Twain**

Going to a funeral is like eating chicken at Popeye's. People are wearing hats, everyone stands around in a crowd, and what you want comes in a box.

☎ . . . . **Jared Krichevsky**

The proof that we don't understand death is that we give the dead people a suit and a pillow. If you can't stretch out and get some solid rest at that point, I don't think there are any bedding accessories that can make any difference. What situation are you going into with a suit and a pillow? There's no business nap meetings.

☎ . . . . Jerry Seinfeld

I was leaving a funeral home when a man approached me and said, "Rabbi, your eulogy for my aunt was wonderful. She would have loved it. And to think, what a shame. She missed it by just two days."

☎ . . . . Rabbi Bob Alper

Gambling

I used to be a heavy gambler. Now I just make mental bets. That's how I lost my mind.

☎ . . . . Steve Allen

I don't get no respect. I joined Gamblers Anonymous. They gave me two to one I don't make it.

☎ . . . . . Rodney Dangerfield

Games

I think it's wrong that only one company makes the game Monopoly.

☎ . . . . Steven Wright

Gardening

If you water it and it dies, it's a plant. If you pull it out and it grows back, it's a weed.

☎ . . . . **Gallagher**

I do not have a green thumb. I can't even get mold to grow on last month's takeout.

☎ . . . **Johnnye Jones Gibson**

Gasoline

Dick Cheney announced more development of domestic coal, gas, and oil. It should have no effect on your quality of living as long as you live in a burrow under the earth.

☎ . . . . **Steve Carell**

Gas is going to three dollars a gallon. I never thought I'd be paying more for my gas than for my wine.

☎ . . . . **David Letterman**

Gas prices are so high in Chicago, cab drivers are taking the real way to the airport.

☎ . . . . **Jay Leno**

Gasoline may go to three dollars a gallon to cover the ever-increasing cost of screwing us.

☎ . . . . **Craig Kilborn**

It looks like Exxon is going to buy Mobil Oil. Their goal is to create the largest chain of filthy rest rooms in the world.

☎ . . . . **Jay Leno**

Gays

They say you can't tell guys are gay just by looking. But if two guys are kissing, you can figure at least one of them is gay.

☎ . . . . **Bill Braudis**

Some men think that they can convert gay women, make them straight. I couldn't do that. I could make a straight woman gay, though.

☎ . . . . **Jeff Stilson**

My brother is gay and my parents don't care, as long as he marries a doctor.

☎ . . . . **Elayne Boosler**

I came out to a straight friend and told her I'm a lesbian. The first thing she said to me was, "Really? Do you know Jill McGee? She's a lesbian in Philadelphia." Pardon me for laughing, but straight people are so funny! They think we all know each other. Actually, I do know her. But, hey, it's just a coincidence.

☎ . . . . **Karen Ripley**

A study claims that the relative lengths of the index and ring fingers indicate whether a woman is a lesbian. If between her thumb and index finger is another woman's nipple, that's an even better indication.

☎ . . . . **Bill Maher**

My grandmother actually knew I was gay before I did. I really didn't know. My grandmother turned to me, in her Yiddish accent, she says, "So, Judy, what? Are you a homosectional?" I thought that was something you bought in department stores, "I'd like two end tables, and that lovely homosectional."

☎ .... **Judy Carter**

The Kinsey Institute says gay men have bigger sex organs. Hence the origin of gay pride.

☎ .... **Jay Leno**

Lots of people think that bisexual *means cowardly lesbian.*

☎ **Sandra Bernhard**

Labels can be misleading. I saw a news report about a lesbian protest march, and the reporter said, "Coming up next, a lesbian demonstration." My first thought was, "Cool. I always wondered how those things work."

☎ .... **Michael Dane**

Being gay has never really been that big of a deal for me. Even my mother, who still lives in Louisville, Kentucky, has taken it quite well. She can have visitors now. Not every day, and just a few at a time, the rooms are so small where they keep her now.

☎ .... **Barry Steiger**

I don't even consider myself bisexual. I just think of myself as a "people person."

☎ .... **Michael Dane**

I was a teenage lesbian. And while that may sound like a horror movie to some of you, I could subtitle that period of my life "Adventures in Paradise" because there was one thing that gay teenagers could do that our straight friends couldn't. I could say, "Hey, Mom, Michelle's comin' over to spend the night Friday, okay?" "Okay, Honey!"

☎ .... **Marilyn Pittman**

I was performing at a comedy club, and when I said I'm a lesbian, a guy in the audience yelled out, "Can I watch?" I said, "Watch me what? Fix my car?"

☎ .... **Sabrina Matthews**

The radical right is so homophobic that they're blaming global warming on the AIDS quilt.

☎ .... **Dennis Miller**

They say having gays in the military would hurt morale. No, it won't. Look: You're in a foxhole, under heavy fire. Don't you think the guy next to you is more likely to save your life if he's in love with you?

☎ .... **Dylan Brody**

Two gay men have given two million dollars to their college's Gay, Lesbian, Bisexual, and Transgender Center. In my day we just called it Drama Club.

☎ .... **Jay Leno**

Gifts

The best stocking stuffer is a human leg.

☎ .... **Norm Macdonald**

There's an entire industry of bad gifts. All those "execu-tIve" gifts, any stupid, goofy, brass wood thing, they put a piece of green felt on the bottom, "It's a gold-desk-tie-stress-organizer, Dad."

☎ .... **Jerry Seinfeld**

Girl Scouts

I was expelled from the Girl Scouts for creativity. They had another name for it: pyromania.

☎ .... **Aurora Cotsbeck**

God

In the beginning there was nothing. God said, "Let there be light!" And there was light. There was still nothing, but you could see it a whole lot better.

☎ .... **Ellen DeGeneres**

I dreamed that God sneezed and I didn't know what to say to him.

☎ .... **Henny Youngman**

If only God would give me some clear sign! Like making a large deposit in my name at a Swiss bank.

☎ .... **Woody Allen**

War, disease, death, destruction, hunger, filth, poverty, torture, crime, corruption, and the Ice Capades. If this is the best God can do, I'm not impressed. Results like these do not belong on the résumé of a supreme being. This is the kind of stuff you'd expect from an office temp with a bad attitude.

☎ .... **George Carlin**

I believe there is something out there watching us. Unfortunately, it's the government.

☎ .... **Woody Allen**

And God said, "Let there be Satan so people don't blame everything on Me. And let there be lawyers, so people don't blame everything on Satan."

☎ .... **John Wing**

And God said, "Let the earth bring forth grass, and the earth brought forth grass and the Rastafarians smoked it."

☎ .... **Spike Milligan**

And when God, who created the entire universe with all of its glories, decides to deliver a message to humanity, He will not use, as His messenger, a person on cable TV with a bad hairstyle.

☎ .... **Dave Barry**

> *I think God's going to come down and pull civilization over for speeding.*
>
> ☎ **Steven Wright**

A Pennsylvania man is suing God. He blamed God for losing his job. The case was thrown out because God does not have access to legal counsel. There are no lawyers in heaven.

☎ . . . . **Jay Leno**

God's got more phonies claiming to know His will than Howard Hughes. Jerry Falwell says homosexuality and abortion are sins. Yeah, so is gluttony, Jerry, so why don't you drop fifty pounds or so?

☎ . . . . **Dennis Miller**

Suicide is man's way of telling God, "You can't fire me, I quit."

☎ . . . . **Bill Maher**

Golf

If you watch a game, it's fun. If you play it, it's recreation. If you work at it, it's golf.

☎ . . . . **Bob Hope**

Golf is one of the few sports where a white man can dress like a black pimp.

☎ . . . . **Robin Williams**

I went to play golf and tried to shoot my age, but I shot my weight instead.

☎ . . . . **Bob Hope**

While playing golf today I hit two good balls. I stepped on a rake.

☎ . . . . **Henny Youngman**

Give me my golf clubs, fresh air, and a beautiful partner, and you can keep my golf clubs and the fresh air.

☎ .... **Jack Benny**

The odd thing about Tiger Woods and a grand slam is that if he went into a Denny's he couldn't even order one.

☎ .... **Bill Maher**

The world's coming to an end. The world's best golfer is black, and the world's best rapper is white.

☎ .... **Chris Rock**

Government

To call our government a cesspool of waste is to do a disservice to all the plucky amoebae out there who thrive on human excrement.

☎ .... **Dennis Miller**

Worst Case Scenario: The U.S. budget written by, or rather as told to, George W. Bush.

☎ .... **Jon Stewart**

The U.S. Treasury unveiled a new quarter that features a special design honoring New York. The New York quarter features illustrations of the Statue of Liberty, the Hudson River, and a taxi driver running over his mother.

☎ .... **Conan O'Brien**

If you want to put an end to government spending, don't pay our president, senators, and representatives a salary. Give them 10 percent of our tax refunds every year. In three months, the entire federal bureaucracy would be run out of a windowless basement in Georgetown by a ninety-year-old guy named Frankie with an unlisted rotary-dial phone.

☎ . . . . **Dennis Miller**

Census workers have been attacked by people they're trying to interview. No one knows how many.

☎ . . . . **Jon Stewart**

George W. Bush went into a think tank this week and almost drowned.

☎ . . . . **Jay Leno**

At the Department of Justice there was a statue of a half-naked woman. The White House decided to cover the statue up. So they covered it with one of J. Edgar Hoover's dresses.

☎ . . . . **David Letterman**

Government pay is so abysmally low, many politicians these days supplement their income by giving talks. For instance, Mario Cuomo makes about twenty thousand dollars per speech, Oliver North gets up to twenty-five thousand dollars an hour, and Bob Packwood gets $3.95 a minute.

☎ . . . . **Bill Maher**

A copy of the Declaration of Independence is being auctioned over the Internet. The copy has never been handled and, judging by events, seldom been read.

☎ . . . . **Jon Stewart**

San Francisco is going to pay for city employees who want sex changes. The city will save money though. After they change a man to a woman, they only have to pay her 75 percent of what he was making. The HMO version is a sock to stuff down your pants and a remote control. "Okay, you're a guy."

☎ . . . . **Jay Leno**

Grandparents

The reason grandparents and grandchildren get along so well is that they have a common enemy.

☎ . . . . **Sam Levenson**

My grandfather is a little forgetful, and he likes to give me advice. One day he took me aside, and left me there.

☎ . . . . **Ron Richards**

I got my grandmother a Seeing Eye dog, but he's a little sadistic. He does impressions of cars screeching to a halt.

☎ . . . . **Larry Amoros**

I was raised by my grandparents, which isn't always fun. They eat dinner very early. It got earlier and earlier. It started at five. Then it was four. Then it was 3:30. One year we had Thanksgiving dinner August 17th, but at least it was a Thursday.

☎ . . . . **Dobie Maxwell**

Gratification

Instant gratification takes too long.

☎ . . . . **Carrie Fisher**

Gravity

It's a good thing we have gravity, or else when birds died they'd just stay right up there. Hunters would be all confused.

☎ . . . . **Steven Wright**

Guns

They say guns don't kill people; people kill people. But I think the guns help. Just standing there saying *bang* doesn't really hurt anybody.

☎ . . . . **Eddie Izzard**

I'm all for gun control. Sometimes I shake a little; I've got to use two hands.

☎ . . . . **Tom Kearney**

Charlton Heston was speaking at Brandeis University. He was wearing a Guns N' Moses T-shirt. Like all National Rifle Association leaders, Heston's blood type is cold.

☎ . . . . **Jon Stewart**

The NRA announced they're opening a "family-oriented" theme restaurant in Times Square "to show the good side of guns." That would be the back side. In front, it's awful.

☎ . . . . **Jon Stewart**

They keep saying assault weapons can be used as legitimate hunting rifles. Okay, I can buy that. You can also use a chain saw to cut butter. It's just going to get a little messy around muffin time.

☎ . . . . **Will Durst**

There's a group in D.C. called the Pink Pistols, and they're pro-gay and pro-gun. They want no waiting period to buy firearms at the Pottery Barn. Their favorite TV hour is *Will & Grace* followed by *Just Shoot Me.* Their motto is, "Yes, that *is* a gun in our pocket, and we *are* happy to see you."

☎ . . . . **Jay Leno**

Why do I need a gun license? It's only for use around the house.

☎ **Charles Addams**

Of course we need firearms. You never know when some nut is going to come up to you and say something like, "You're fired." You gotta be ready.

☎ . . . . **Dave Attell**

Gyms

Any day that you had gym was a weird school day. It started off normal; English, geometry, social studies, and then suddenly you're in *Lord of the Flies* for forty minutes. You're hanging from a rope; you have hardly any clothes on. Kids are throwing dodge balls at you, snapping towels; you're trying to survive. And then it's history, science, language. There's something off in the whole flow of that day.

☎ . . . . **Jerry Seinfeld**

According to a study of health clubs, men sweat more than women. Well, sure. It takes a lot more effort to hold in their gut for an hour.

☎ . . . . **Jay Leno**

Hair

I just had my hair cut. They cut my hair too short, and now I can't get it to do what I want it to. I want it to type.

☎ . . . . **Paula Poundstone**

Women definitely go to maintenance extremes. One of the great mysteries to me is the fact that a woman could pour hot wax on her legs, rip the hair out by the roots, and still be afraid of a spider.

☎ . . . . **Jerry Seinfeld**

Nobody is really happy with what's on their head. People with straight hair want curly, people with curly want straight, and bald people want everyone to be blind.

☎ . . . . **Rita Rudner**

I must be going bald. It's taking longer and longer to wash my face.

☎ . . . . **Harry Hill**

I don't consider myself bald. I'm simply taller than my hair.

☎ . . . . **Thom Sharp**

As soon as my hair started to fall out I asked my girlfriend to marry me. I figured I'd better lock and load while I still had the option.

☎ . . . . **Greg Fitzsimmons**

For men, the hair transplant is an interesting process. Hair that was on your shower soap yesterday can be in your head tomorrow. How did they do the first transplant? Did they have the guy take a shower, get his soap, rush it to the hospital by helicopter, keep the soap alive on a soap support system? "We got the hairs, but I think we lost the Zest."

☎ . . . . **Jerry Seinfeld**

A tip for you: If you have no hair, people can tell you're bald. If you have no hair, and you order spray paint to put on your head, people can tell you're bald, and a moron.

☎ . . . . **Dylan Brody**

Gray hair is God's graffiti.

☎ . . . . **Bill Cosby**

Happiness

What's the use of happiness?
It can't buy you money.

☎ ...... **Henny Youngman**

Money can't buy you happiness, but it does bring you a
more pleasant form of misery.

☎ .... **Spike Milligan**

Health Care

In the health care area, the
Republicans have unveiled
their "Get Tough on Sick
People" policy.

☎ .... **Stephen Colbert**

Some people have physicians
who are in an HMO or a PPO.
Mine are in a UFO: You want
to believe they exist, but
there's really no evidence.

☎ .... **Reno Goodale**

Health Clubs

On what machine at a health
club would you be most
likely to meet a super
model? The ATM machine.

☎ .... **Jay Leno**

History

I was terrible at history. I could never see the point of learning what people thought back when people were a lot stupider. For instance, the ancient Phoenicians believed that the sun was carried across the sky on the back of an enormous snake. So what? So they were idiots.

☎ . . . . **Dave Barry**

Do you know the real reason Abraham Lincoln was shot in the theater? His cell phone kept going off.

☎ . . . . **Jay Leno**

If you think you have it tough, read history books.

☎ . . . . **Bill Maher**

Hobbies

I've been working out lately; it's my new hobby. I thought I already had a hobby, but apparently going out, getting stinking drunk, and giving creepy guys phony phone numbers is not actually considered a hobby, but a "lifestyle."

☎ . . . . **Andi Rhoads**

There is a very fine line between "hobby" and "mental illness."

☎ . . . . **Dave Barry**

Holidays

You can tell it's the Christmas season. Stores are selling off their expired milk as eggnog.

☎ . . . . **David Letterman**

I was an elf for the mall Santa. Turns out nothing can get you out of the Christmas spirit quite like children. One lollipop stuck in your hair, and you find yourself saying, "This year for Christmas, Santa is bringing you a big box of *death*."

☎ . . . . , **Kris McGaha**

Santa is very jolly because he knows where all the bad girls live.

☎ . . . . **Dennis Miller**

Christmas in California is very different from the rest of the country. Out here, the Santas don't look the same. You know, the liposuction, the fanny tucks. And Los Angeles Santas don't park on your roof: They valet.

☎ . . . . **Jay Leno**

I never believed in Santa Claus because I knew no white dude would come into my neighborhood after dark.

☎ . . . . **Dick Gregory**

I used to work in a Fotomat booth. Talk about the world's worst office Christmas party. I sat in a mall parking lot with a punchbowl and a candy cane.

☎ **Dobie Maxwell**

Last Christmas I got no respect. I gave my kid a BB gun. He gave me a sweatshirt with a bull's-eye in the back.

☎ . . . . . **Rodney Dangerfield**

I have figured out a good way to get rid of your Christmas tree. Do what I did. Put a price tag on it, drag it to the curb, and wait for Winona Ryder to come by and take it.

☎ . . . . **Craig Kilborn**

I haven't taken my Christmas lights down. They look so nice on the pumpkin.

☎ . . . . **Winston Spear**

Mexican people celebrate Cinco de Mayo to commemorate their defeat of the French. Hasn't everybody beat the French? Let them beat the Germans. Then they can celebrate. Think if the French had won. Then we'd have illegal immigrants who are also rude.

☎ . . . . **Jay Leno**

On Columbus Day, Native Americans put out ice cream and cake, and then watch the white people take it from them.

☎ . . . . **Conan O'Brien**

Today is Columbus Day. Columbus is the guy who, except for the Indians, the Vikings, the Egyptians, and possibly the space aliens, discovered America.

☎ . . . . **Craig Kilborn**

On Halloween I ran out of candy and had to give the kids nicotine gum.

☎ . . . . **David Letterman**

When I was a kid my parents always sent me out as a tramp: high-heel shoes, fishnet stockings …

☎ .... **David Letterman**

Don't forget Mother's Day. Or as they call it in Beverly Hills, Dad's Third Wife Day.

☎ .... **Jay Leno**

As you know, Labor Day is the day when we honor hard-working people in America. So let's take a moment to thank all those people by saying, "Gracias, amigos!"

☎ .... **Jay Leno**

Super Bowl Sunday is the one day of the year where everyone in the country, regardless of their religious beliefs, completely stops what they're normally doing. Especially the team I'm rooting for.

☎ .... **Dennis Miller**

Mother's Day is the biggest day of the year for long-distance telephone calls. Makes you wonder why so many people move long distances from Mom, doesn't it? I'm off the hook this year, though. Mom thinks I'm still in the hospital.

☎ .... **David Letterman**

The crime rate goes down during the Super Bowl. Of course. All the players are on the field. Football's like Congress. You're just working with a different group of felons.

☎ .... **Jay Leno**

Thanksgiving, when the Indians said, "Well, this has been fun, but we know you have a long voyage back to England."

☎ .... **Jay Leno**

Thanksgiving is the day when you turn to another family member and say, "How long has Mom been drinking like this?" My mom, after six Bloody Marys, looks at the turkey and goes, "Here, kitty, kitty."

☎ .... **David Letterman**

Thanksgiving is an emotional time. People travel thousands of miles to be with people they only see once a year. And then discover once a year is way too often.

☎ .... **Johnny Carson**

Whales, they're great for Thanksgiving, but a real bitch to stuff.

☎ .... **Craig Kilborn**

You can tell you ate too much for Thanksgiving when you have to let your bathrobe out.

☎ .... **Jay Leno**

Women get a little more excited about New Year's Eve than men do. It's like an excuse, you get drunk, you make a lot of promises you're not going to keep, the next morning as soon as you wake up you start breaking them. For men, we just call that a date.

☎ .... **Jay Leno**

Thanksgiving, when we all count our blessings. And the real Thanksgiving is Sunday when you drive all your relatives to the airport.

☎ .... **David Letterman**

A hundred members of the Polar Bear Club celebrated New Year's Day by swimming in the freezing waters of the Atlantic Ocean. Then later that afternoon, all the men joined the I-Can't-Find-My-Testicles Club.

☎ .... **Conan O'Brien**

I don't understand why Cupid was chosen to represent Valentine's Day. When I think about romance, the last thing on my mind is a short, chubby toddler coming at me with a weapon.

☎ .... **Paul McGinty**

Hallmark is coming out with a new card for guys who forget Valentine's Day. The card is small and gold and maxes out at ten grand.

☎ .... **Craig Kilborn**

On May 1, Worker's Day, Indonesian Nike employees were brought out for their annual look at the sun.

☎ .... **Jay Leno**

On May Day, anticapitalist protesters in London tore down the golden arches of a McDonald's. Then they put them up again when they realized it was the best food in Britain.

☎ .... **Jon Stewart**

Honesty

I was walking down Fifth Avenue today and I found a wallet. I was gonna keep it, rather than return it. But I thought: Well, if I lost a hundred and fifty dollars, how would I feel? And I realized I would want to be taught a lesson.

☎ . . . . **Emo Philips**

Hotels

I saw a billboard for a small hotel that said, "We Treat You Like Family." And sure enough, nine o'clock the next morning, someone was banging on my door yelling, "When the hell are you gonna get a place of your own?"

☎ . . . . **Brian McKim**

Hotels and I appear to differ on the precise definition of what constitutes a non-smoking room. Hotels' definition appears to be "Nobody's smoking in there right now." Two months ago in New York, I stayed in a nonsmoking room that smelled like the guy before had been curing a ham.

☎ . . . . **Dennis Miller**

A hotel is a place that keeps the manufacturers of twenty-five-watt bulbs in business.

☎ . . . . **Shelley Berman**

In San Francisco somebody wants to build a replica of the *Titanic* and use it as a hotel. Instead of having to go down the hall for ice, the ice would come to you.

☎ . . . . **Conan O'Brien**

Housework

I do clean up a little. If company is coming, I'll wipe the lipstick off the milk container.

☎ . . . . **Elayne Boosler**

We're single guys, nobody washes dishes. I had to go to the closet and get the Yahtzee game, to find a clean cup to drink out of.

☎ . . . . **Dobie Maxwell**

I buried a lot of my ironing in the backyard.

☎ . . . . **Phyllis Diller**

My mother is a clean freak. She vacuumed so much, the guy downstairs went bald.

☎ . . . . **Steve Bridges**

Housing

I live in your standard no-frills apartment. Just the basics: water, electricity, and more roaches than I'll ever be able to kill in a lifetime. Not that I've been able to kill any. I've had so many of them check out of the roach motel, I've had to hire a night clerk to help them with the luggage.

☎ . . . . **Andi Rhoads**

I can't believe I actually own my own house. I'm looking at a house; it's two hundred grand. The Realtor says, "It's got a great view." For two hundred grand I better open up the curtains and see breasts against the window.

☎ . . . . **Garry Shandling**

Humanity

I had a linguistics professor who said that it's man's ability to use language that makes him the dominant species on the planet. I think there's one other thing that separates us from animals: We aren't afraid of vacuum cleaners.

☎ . . . . **Jeff Stilson**

If you had to identify, in one word, the reason why the human race has not and never will achieve its full potential, that word would be: *meetings.*

☎ . . . . **Dave Barry**

I think I am a pretty good judge of people, which is why I hate most of them.

☎ . . . . **Roseanne**

Humidifiers

I filled the humidifier with wax and left it on. Now everything in my house is shiny.

☎ . . . . **Steven Wright**

Hypothetical

Imagine if there were no hypothetical situations.

☎ . . . . **John Mendosa**

Illness

First the doctor told me the good news: I was going to have a disease named after me.

☎ . . . . **Steve Martin**

If Dick Cheney has one more incident, he may have to have his heart removed. Luckily, he can still be a Republican.

☎ . . . . **Craig Kilborn**

It was reported that sex is good for people with arthritis. It's just not that pleasant to watch.

☎ . . . . **Jay Leno**

I admit it; I'm a hypochondriac. But I manage to control it with a placebo.

☎ . . . . **Dennis Miller**

Got my flu shot a month ago, been sick ever since. What a racket that is. I should have known something was up when my shot came with a coupon for cough syrup.

☎ . . . . **Tom Kearney**

You can always tell when it's cold and flu season: You go to the Sizzler and can't see the salad through the sneeze guard.

☎ . . . . **Jay Leno**

Ever get one of those ice cream headaches? You know, when you tell your girlfriend she's gaining weight, and she hits you with the scoop? "Ow! I said that too fast!"

☎ . . . . **Jeff Shaw**

Incense

What's the deal with incense? It smells like somebody set fire to a clothes hamper. Gym socks and jasmine. Do we need that smell? You know what incense smells like? If flowers could fart.

☎ . . . . **Billiam Coronel**

Insects

Ants can carry twenty times their own body weight, which is useful information if you're moving and you need help carrying a potato chip across town.

☎ . . . . **Ron Darian**

I don't kill flies, but I like to mess with their minds. I hold them above globes. They freak out and yell, "Whoa, I'm way too high!"

☎ . . . . **Bruce Baum**

A study has shown most men will eat food a fly has landed on, while most women won't. I won't eat any food a fly *won't* land on.

☎ . . . . **Jay Leno**

The stick insect has sex for seventy-nine days straight. If it's only been seventy-seven days, is that a quickie? And you know that even after seventy-nine days, the female goes, "Oh, so close!" And the guy tells his buddies it was 158 days.

☎ . . . . **Jay Leno**

A seventy-seven-year-old woman in Las Vegas was attacked by killer bees. It took a fire hose to get the bees off her, and a crowbar to pry her hand from the slot machine handle.

☎ . . . . **Bill Maher**

We hope that, when the insects take over the world, they will remember with gratitude how we took them along on our picnics.

☎ . . . . **Bill Vaughan**

Insurance

I used to sell life insurance. But life insurance is a really weird concept. You really don't get anything for it. It works like this: You pay *me* money. And when you die, I'll pay *you* money.

☎ . . . . **Bill Kirchenbauer**

Insurance is a uniquely modern atrocity. At the dawn of man, there was no insurance. You either lived or died. There was no fast-grunting biped called *Homo deductus* demanding a piece of your meat every month to guarantee that your fire wouldn't go out.

☎ . . . . **Dennis Miller**

There's a plan to allow banks to merge with insurance companies. This would produce a new race of super-boring human beings.

☎ . . . . **Jay Leno**

Intelligence

Is the average person stupider today than he was a generation ago? Or do you just run into more stupid people because fewer stupid people are getting eaten by bears?

☎ . . . . **Bill Maher**

I lived down south in Alabama for two years when I was in the Army. And I can tell you now that if ignorance is bliss, than an Alabama redneck is Buddha.

☎ . . . . **Eric Fleming**

Aren't people stupid? Not us, it's the others. Ever notice that when you're with someone and they taste something bad, they want you to taste it, too? "This is disgusting! It's gross! Taste this, taste how bad it is!" And we're stupid, we taste it. "All right. I'm going to vomit!"

☎ . . . . **Ellen DeGeneres**

There's a new telephone 800 or 900 number where you can call and test your IQ. It costs $3.95 a minute. I understand the test is pretty simple: If you call at all you're an idiot; if you stay on for three minutes or more you're a moron.

☎ . . . . **Jay Leno**

Internet

When I log on to AOL it says, "You've got problems."

☎ . . . . **Richard Lewis**

Computer hackers broke into Yahoo, the Internet's most popular Web site, and vowed to unleash a crippling computer virus if a fellow hacker is not released from prison. Experts warn that catching these cyber terrorists will not be an easy task, and may require the cooperation of both nerds *and* geeks.

☎ . . . . **Norm Macdonald**

You can e-mail me, but I prefer letters that come through conventional mail. I like letters that have been licked by strangers.

☎ . . . . **David Letterman**

Did you see where eBay wouldn't let this guy auction off his soul? They said, "If you want to sell your soul, you'll just have to run for president like everybody else."

☎ . . . . **Jay Leno**

eBay was shut down for three hours, leading to a loss of six million dollars' worth of sales of useless crap.

☎ . . . . **Colin Quinn**

Many online businesses have closed, but the Internet still offers abundant options to discriminating shoppers, as long as what they want is porn.

☎ . . . . **Vance DeGeneres**

The Supreme Court ruled in favor of pornography on the Internet. Then, after the ruling, there was an awkward moment when Clarence Thomas started high-fiving everybody.

☎ . . . . **Conan O'Brien**

Congress says that half of Americans use the Internet. The other half has sex with real partners.

☎ . . . . **Jay Leno**

The Web brings people together because no matter what kind of a twisted sexual mutant you happen to be, you've got millions of pals out there. Type in "Find people who have sex with goats that are on fire," and the computer will say, "Specify type of goat."

☎ . . . . **Richard Jeni**

I found this site where models are selling their eggs over the Internet. Oh great, that's what this world needs, more vanity. Not more Einsteins or Picassos, more anorexic, catwalking hat racks.

☎ .... **Kris McGaha**

A common criticism of the Internet is that it is dominated by the crude, the uninformed, the immature, the smug, the untalented, the repetitious, the pathetic, the hostile, the deluded, the self-righteous, and the shrill. This criticism overlooks the fact that the Internet also offers, for the savvy individual who knows where to look, the tasteless and the borderline insane.

☎ .... **Dave Barry**

A drug company is in trouble for selling Viagra to an eleven-year-old over the Internet. His mother said, "Don't run with that, Johnny. You'll poke someone's eye out."

☎ .... **Craig Kilborn**

My favorite thing about the Internet is that you get to go into the private world of real creeps without having to smell them.

☎ .... **Penn Jillette**

Computer-industry repre-sentatives have agreed that "family control" technology on the Internet already exists. It's just that kids won't explain it to their parents.

☎ .... **Craig Kilborn**

Intimacy

My friends tell me I have an intimacy problem. But they don't really know me.

☎ . . . . **Garry Shandling**

Inventions

My father invented the burglar alarm, which unfortunately was stolen from him.

☎ . . . . **Victor Borge**

The people who invented nonalcoholic beer are working on liver without vitamins.

☎ . . . . **Elayne Boosler**

Some guy's invented a portable bidet. And you were annoyed by people using their cell phones in public.

☎ . . . . **Jay Leno**

I have a friend who's a billionaire; he invented Cliff Notes. When I asked him how he got such a great idea, he said, "Well, to make a long story short . . ."

☎ . . . . **Steven Wright**

The creator of Cliff Notes has died. George W. Bush said, "He was my favorite author."

☎ . . . . **Conan O'Brien**

The inventor of Crest passed away. Four out of five dentists came to the funeral.

☎ . . . . **Jay Leno**

My uncle invented a laundry detergent for chain-smokers. You throw it in with your laundry, and it makes your clothes smell like a fresh pack of cigarettes.

☎ . . . . **Wally Wang**

In Thailand they're turning elephant dung into wrapping paper. Takes the special feeling out of getting a gift, doesn't it?

☎ . . . . **Jay Leno**

If it weren't for electricity we'd all be watching television by candlelight.

☎ . . . . **George Gobel**

I invented the cordless extension cord.

☎ . . . . **Steven Wright**

Fahrenheit was born on this day in 1686. He was an annoying man. It was by asking people what he should do with his invention that he discovered the rectal thermometer.

☎ . . . . **Jay Leno**

My uncle invented the solar-powered funeral home. He's got basic solar technology, big solar panels on the roof, the sun beats down, it heats up the panels. Trouble is, he can't cremate, he can only poach.

☎ . . . . **Heywood Banks**

Who invented the brush they put next to the toilet? That thing hurts!

☎ . . . . **Andy Andrews**

Robert Tools, the world's first recipient of a self-contained heart, admitted that the device was very expensive, but it comes with unlimited weekend minutes.

☎ . . . . **Bill Maher**

A woman in Minneapolis has invented a product called Bodyperks, a pair of silicon nipple enhancers that make women's nipples continually look erect. Not surprisingly, she's being sued by the man who invented air-conditioning.

☎ . . . . **Conan O'Brien**

To celebrate the anniversary of the invention of sandpaper, Kmart is offering half off on their house-brand toilet paper.

☎ . . . . **Jay Leno**

Investments

My accountant told me to invest two thousand dollars a year in an IRA. I just found out this year they're losing that war.

☎ . . . . **Buzz Nutley**

Jobs

Here's some advice. At a job interview tell them you're willing to give 110 percent. Unless the job is statistician.

☎ . . . . **Adam Gropman**

I used to work at a health food store. I got fired for drinking straight Bosco on the job.

☎ . . . . **Steven Wright**

I used to sell furniture for a living. The trouble was, it was my own.

☎ .... **Les Dawson**

My first job was on a suicide hotline. That was tough, because every time I tried to call in sick, my boss would talk me out of it.

☎ .... **Wally Wang**

There are many ways to know that you have a bad job. For instance, if you have to carry out the body of the guy whose place you're taking. Or, if you're employed at the post office next to a coworker who's constantly muttering under his breath, and the only word you can make out is your name.

☎ .... **Dennis Miller**

Half of Americans say they've had sex on the job. No wonder foreign workers are trying to sneak into the country.

☎ .... **Jay Leno**

I used to be a proofreader for a skywriting company.

☎ .... **Steven Wright**

The chalk outline guy's got a good job. Not too dangerous, the criminals are long gone. I guess these were people who wanted to be sketch artists, but they couldn't draw very well. "Uh, listen, Jon, forget the sketches. Do you think if we left the dead body right there on the side-walk, you could manage to trace around it?"

☎ .... **Jerry Seinfeld**

The University of Illinois has hired fifteen women to smell pig manure all day so that researchers can find out what makes pig manure smell so bad. You know who I feel sorry for? The woman who applied for this job and got turned down.

☎ .... **Jay Leno**

Juggling

Some people think a juggler is talented. Could be a schizophrenic playing catch.

☎ .... **Bob Dubac**

Kissing

Kissing is just pushing your lips against the sweet end of sixty-six feet of intestines.

☎ .... **Drew Carey**

Knives

Swiss Army Knives got their name because it takes the entire Swiss Army just to carry one.

☎ .... **Nick Arnette**

Knowledge

Everybody is ignorant, only on different subjects.

☎ .... **Will Rogers**

Laundry

I hate going to the Laundromat in my last clean clothes on the planet. Two months ago I went down there in my Boy Scout uniform. I was all embarrassed, until another guy came in wearing his graduation cap and gown.

☎ . . . . **Dobie Maxwell**

Lawsuits

Adolf Hitler's nieces and nephews are suing for twenty million dollars for royalties on *Mein Kampf*. I hope this unseemly squabbling doesn't tarnish the Hitler family name. But maybe his relatives should pay for the damage Uncle Adolf did on his little European book tour.

☎ . . . . **Jay Leno**

Puff Daddy is being sued for two million dollars in a paternity suit. Puffy denied paternity, saying he may have been in the room when it happened, but he never fired his weapon.

☎ . . . . **Conan O'Brien**

Jerry Garcia's estate is being sued by his personal trainer. Shouldn't it be the other way around? When Ben & Jerry name an ice cream flavor after your client, I think his estate should sue you.

☎ . . . . **Jay Leno**

Continental is being sued by a family that had a dead guy next to them on a flight. He'd used his frequent-flier miles to upgrade from cargo.

☎ . . . . **David Letterman**

Cracker Barrel restaurants is getting sued $150 million for having a racially insensitive name. In response, Cracker Barrel has announced they are changing their name to the Redneck Barrel.

☎ .... **Jay Leno**

A Tiffany employee was suing her bosses for abuse and humiliation. So basically, they were treating her like one of their customers.

☎ .... **David Letterman**

O.J. is still fighting the judgment against him by Fred Goldman for thirty-two million dollars. He was in court again and said to the judge, "I can't pay this. I'm a murderer, not a thief!"

☎ .... **Jay Leno**

Lawyers

Yale gave George W. Bush an honorary law degree. Now he's an honorary lawyer, the same way he's an honorary president.

☎ .... **David Letterman**

Leadership

When trouble arises and things look bad, there is always one individual who perceives a solution and is willing to take command. Very often, that individual is crazy.

☎ .... **Dave Barry**

Libraries

I get no respect. I was crossing the street, I got hit by a mobile library. I was lying there in pain, screaming. The guy looked at me and went, "Shhhh."

☎ ..... **Rodney Dangerfield**

Life

I like life. It's something to do.

☎ .... **Ronnie Shakes**

Life's a bitch. Then you marry one.

☎ .... **Steve Carell**

Life is a sexually transmitted disease.

☎ .... **Guy Bellamy**

Everyone has a purpose in life. Perhaps yours is watching television.

☎ .... **David Letterman**

You can't do anything about the length of your life, but you can do something about its width and depth.

☎ .... **Evan Esar**

I don't want to achieve immortality through my work. I want to achieve it through not dying.

☎ .... **Woody Allen**

Seize the moment. Remember all those women on the *Titanic* who waved off the dessert cart.

☎ .... **Erma Bombeck**

I wanna live till I die, no more, no less.

☎ . . . . **Eddie Izzard**

I intend to live forever. So far, so good.

☎ . . . . **Steven Wright**

Do we really need these new Wonder Pants that do for your butt what the Wonder Bra does for breasts? Do we really need more cleavage down there? I think my plumber has a pair.

☎ . . . . **Jay Leno**

Lingerie

Push-up bras are like breasts on the half-shell.

☎ . . . . **Dom Irrera**

Frederick's of Hollywood has filed for bankruptcy. They're pinning their hopes for recovery on the H2O Bra, filled with water. The bra is perfect for the woman who's thirsty after carrying her luscious breasts around all day.

☎ . . . . **Jon Stewart**

Los Angeles

Fall is my favorite season in Los Angeles, watching the birds change color and fall from the trees.

☎ . . . . **David Letterman**

I'm from Los Angeles. I don't trust any air I can't see.

☎ . . . . **Bob Hope**

I live in Los Angeles. It's kind of scary. What do I do as a parent if someday my son wants to join a gang? Do I carpool drive-by shootings?

☎ . . . . **Robert G. Lee**

Southern California's motto used to be "You are what you eat." Now it's "You are what your lips have been injected with." You can get all your butt fat put into your lips so that every time you talk, you're kissing your own ass. How Hollywood is that?

☎ . . . . **Kate Mason**

If God doesn't destroy Hollywood Boulevard, he owes Sodom and Gomorrah an apology.

☎ . . . . **Jay Leno**

You can't find any true closeness in Hollywood, because everybody does the fake closeness so well.

☎ . . . . **Carrie Fisher**

Love

Love is staying awake all night with a sick child. Or a very healthy adult.

☎ . . . . **Sir David Frost**

My two-year-old nephew says "I love you" to everyone. My sister says he doesn't know what it means. He just says it to get something. I think he knows exactly what it means.

☎ . . . . **Tim Young**

A lot of people wonder how you know if you're really in love. Just ask yourself this one question: "Would I mind being financially destroyed by this person?"

☎ . . . . **Ronnie Shakes**

You can't buy love, but you can pay heavily for it.

☎ . . . . **Henny Youngman**

If love is the answer, could you please rephrase the question?

☎ . . . . **Lily Tomlin**

Magazines

Playboy is coming out with a magazine for married men: every month the same centerfold.

☎ . . . . **Craig Kilborn**

According to *Self* magazine, the tongue is the strongest muscle in the body. Do you think that's true? Let me tell you, if your tongue is the strongest muscle in your body, you need to work out more or shut up.

☎ . . . . **Jay Leno**

This is *Soldier of Fortune*'s twenty-fifth anniversary. That's the magazine read by people while they're crouching behind rocks, shooting paint balls at each other.

☎ . . . . **Jon Stewart**

A mom and dad found an S&M magazine under their ten-year-old son's bed, and the dad said, "Well, we sure can't spank him."

☎ . . . . **Dana Carvey**

Did you ever notice the Playboy Advisor tells you about your love life and your car problems? Do you generally go to the garage and say, "Clem, I'm bothered by sexual dysfunction."

☎ . . . . **Jay Leno**

Women reading *Vogue* magazine about the latest fashions to come off the Paris runway is the same as you men looking at naked women in *Playboy*. We're both looking at places we're never going to visit.

☎ . . . . **Andi Rhoads**

Mail

The other day I got a chain saw in the mail. Now I have to send chain saws to ten other people. The postage alone is gonna kill me.

☎ . . . . **Brian McKim**

Mainstream

The reason the mainstream is thought of as a stream, is because of its shallowness.

☎ . . . . **George Carlin**

Manicures

My girlfriend does her nails with Wite-Out. When she's asleep, I go over there and write misspelled words on them.

☎ . . . . **Steven Wright**

Maps

At home I have a map of the United States, actual size. I spent all summer folding it.

☎ . . . . **Steven Wright**

Marriage

It's historically one of life's most memorable moments, a man asking a woman to marry him. A woman begins to fantasize about what a very special moment it will be. Will he hire a plane to write "Will You Marry Me?" in the sky? And if I don't want to marry him, do I then have to hire a plane to write "No"?

☎ . . . . **Rita Rudner**

Marriage has no guarantees. If that's what you're looking for, go live with a car battery.

☎ . . . . **Erma Bombeck**

Marriage is a wonderful invention. But then again, so is the bicycle repair kit.

☎ . . . . **Billy Connolly**

When we first met, my wife didn't like me all that much. Luckily, she wanted to stay in this country.

☎ . . . . **Brian Kiley**

Many of my friends are getting engaged and are buying diamonds for their fiancées. What better to symbolize marriage than the hardest thing known to man.

☎ . . . . **Mike Dugan**

I think marriage is set up to turn otherwise sexy women into boring drudges. By about the third hand-mixer I was saying to my wedding guests, "Why don't you just include a card that says 'Your life is over'?"

☎ . . . . **Maura Kennedy**

The old saying was "Marry an older man because they're mature." The saying now is "Marry a young man, because men don't mature."

☎ . . . . **Rita Rudner**

My father says, "Marry a girl who has the same belief as the family." I said, "Dad, why would I want a girl who thinks I'm a schmuck?"

☎ . . . . **Adam Sandler**

Men don't feel the urge to get married as quickly as women do because their clothes all button and zip in the front. Women's dresses usually button and zip in the back. We need men emotionally and sexually, but we also need men to help us get dressed.

☎ . . . . **Rita Rudner**

They say, "Settle down and get a wife and kids." How is getting a wife and kids settling down? A marijuana habit is settling down. Having a wife and kids, you better be in the best shape of your life.

☎ **Patrick Keane**

Marriage is real tough because you have to deal with feelings, and lawyers.

☎ .... **Richard Pryor**

I love my husband, I love my children, but I want something more. Like a life.

☎ .... **Roseanne**

I will not cheat on my wife. Because I love my house.

☎ .... **Chas Elstner**

If love means never having to say you're sorry, then marriage means always having to say everything twice. Husbands, due to an unknown quirk of the universe, never hear you the first time.

☎ .... **Estelle Getty**

He tricked me into marrying him. He told me he was pregnant.

☎ .... **Carol Leifer**

Making love while you're married is like being a bad Little League player. Even if you suck, they still have to put you in for two innings.

☎ .... **Buzz Nutley**

You know why Vermont wants gays to get married? To stop them from having sex.

☎ .... **Bill Maher**

My parents have been married for fifty years. I asked my mother how they did it. She said, "You just close your eyes and pretend it's not happening."

☎ .... **Rita Rudner**

Statistics show that the older you are when you get married, the more likely it is you'll stay together. Of course, because at eighty-five you can't hear how boring he is.

☎ ...... **Christine O'Rourke**

Things change when you get married. When I first got married, I would walk around the house with no clothes on. My husband would be like, "Baby, you look so good. Come here." He couldn't keep his hands off me. Now when I walk around the house with no clothes, he's like, "Ain't you cold?"

☎ .... **Roz Browne**

We sleep in separate rooms, we have dinner apart, we take separate vacations. We're doing everything we can to keep our marriage together.

☎ ..... **Rodney Dangerfield**

Our marriage was so bad, our dog died from licking our wedding pictures.

☎ .... **Phyllis Diller**

Measurement

You can measure distance by time. "How far away is it?" "Oh, about twenty minutes." But it doesn't work the other way. "When do you get off work?" "Around three miles."

☎ .... **Jerry Seinfeld**

The metric system did not really catch on in the States, unless you count the increasing popularity of the nine-millimeter bullet.

☎ . . . . **Dave Barry**

Medical Care

More fascinating medical news: Doctors are now starting to use maggots to heal wounds. This doesn't make any sense to me. When was the last time you saw an animal on the side of the road, covered with maggots, that looked like it was getting any better?

☎ . . . . **Jay Leno**

A new study claims that mouth-to-mouth resuscitation is not necessary during CPR and it's better to skip right to chest compression. However, the study says that you're still required to snuggle for a half hour afterwards.

☎ . . . . **Conan O'Brien**

Is alternative medicine really the key to understanding the human body, or is it just a chance to get scammed by some loser who wasn't smart enough to snag the hair-scrunchie franchise at the local mall? While I don't believe traditional medicine has all the answers, it must be pretty frustrating for a Harvard-trained MD to be losing customers to a guy whose sole medical credentials consist of preferring to sit on the floor.

☎ . . . . **Dennis Miller**

A new study indicates that doctors' treatment of whiplash is usually ineffective and can often make the condition worse. According to the study, you're probably better off following your lawyer's advice of applying fresh doses of money on the infected area.

☎ .... **Jay Leno**

I was in the hospital, but I don't think I had the best care. I had this one intern try to get the IV into my arm fifteen times. Finally, they got a junkie from the methadone rehab ward to do it.

☎ .... **Heidi Joyce**

I hope all my blood tests come back as negative as my mother is.

☎ .... **Kate Mason**

Do you know how to avoid overexposure to X rays? Join an HMO.

☎ .... **Jay Leno**

Medication

On the back of a NyQuil bottle it says, "May cause drowsiness." It should say, "Don't make any plans."

☎ .... **Denis Leary**

Five percent of people on antidepressants have orgasms when they yawn. So what the hell do they have to be depressed about?

☎ .... **Jay Leno**

My male roommate and I mixed up our nicotine and testosterone patches. He got cranky and hungry. I got a raise and a corner office.

☎ .... **Karen Ripley**

Drug costs for the elderly are going way up. It now costs 25 percent more to keep Grandma spacey and incoherent.

☎ .... **Craig Kilborn**

I'm addicted to placebos. I'd give them up, but it wouldn't make any difference.

☎ .... **Jay Leno**

Men

Giving a man space is like giving a dog a computer. Chances are he will not use it wisely.

☎ ...... **Bette-Jane Raphael**

Men are simple things. They can survive a whole weekend with only three things: beer, boxer shorts, and batteries for the remote control.

☎ .... **Diana Jordan**

The quickest way to a man's heart is through his chest.

☎ .... **Roseanne**

Men are superior to women. For one thing, men can urinate from a speeding car.

☎ .... **Will Durst**

The only perfect man is Mr. Ed. He's hung like a horse and can hold a conversation.

☎ . . . . **Traci Skene**

Men want Traci Lords in the bedroom, Julia Child in the kitchen, Lesley Visser during a game, Mary Poppins for the children, Cha Cha Muldowney in traffic, Mary Richards at work, Mother Teresa when we come home with leprosy, Gertrude Stein in conversation, the body of Sophia Loren in *Boy on a Dolphin* combined with the voice of Sade, and to top it all off, the IQ of Anna Nicole Smith, because we don't want to feel too threatened.

☎ . . . . **Dennis Miller**

A study shows men are hit by lightning four times as often as women. Usually after saying, "I'll call you."

☎ . . . . **Jay Leno**

Men are only as loyal as their options.

☎ . . . . **Bill Maher**

What are the three words guaranteed to humiliate men everywhere? "Hold my purse."

☎ . . . . **François Morency**

Men are delusional. Hugh Hefner lounges around in a bathrobe with three live-in girlfriends. You know guys are sitting at home watching the Playboy channel and thinking, "That could be me. *I've* got a bathrobe."

☎ . . . . **Denise Robb**

Men think that women like guys who are dangerous. As a result, guys will often smoke cigarettes, drink too much, and ride a motorcycle without a helmet. The reality? Women don't like guys who are dangerous. They want us to think that because women are trying to kill us.

☎ . . . . **Dennis Miller**

A good man doesn't just happen. They have to be created by us women. A guy is a lump, like a donut. So first, you gotta get rid of all the stuff his mom did to him. And then you gotta get rid of all that macho stuff they pick up from beer commercials. And then there's my personal favorite, the male ego.

☎ . . . . **Roseanne**

They say men get sexier as they get older. No, sexy men get sexier as they get older; the rest of us get red sports cars.

☎ . . . . **Jeff Shaw**

Men and women belong to different species, and communication between them is a science still in its infancy.

☎ . . . . **Bill Cosby**

Menstruation

I needed a pint of Ben & Jerry's Super Fudge Chunk and a box of tampons. Pretty much if you're shopping for one, you're shopping for the other. The cashier checked me out and asked, "Paper or plastic?" I said, "Oh, I don't want a bag. I just want to walk down the street with these things out in front of me, and watch people get out of my way."

☎ .... **Sabrina Matthews**

Mental Illness

The Centers for Disease Control in Atlanta, Georgia, announces that they've found a cure for manic depression. I don't know whether to laugh or cry!

☎ .... **Jay Leno**

Merchandise

I bought an irregular electric blanket. It's solar-powered.

☎ .... **Nick Arnette**

Military

Being in the Army is like being in the Boy Scouts, except that the Boy Scouts have adult supervision.

☎ .... **Blake Clark**

The Army is now taking high school dropouts, as part of their "Don't ask, can't spell" policy. They've had to change their slogan to "We do more before the big hand is on the twelve, and the little hand ..."

☎ .... **Jay Leno**

There's the stealth plane, the invisible plane. What good is an invisible airplane going to do? The enemy looks down on their radar and says, "Well, there's no aircraft here. But there's two little guys in a sitting position at forty thousand feet."

☎ .... **Will Durst**

Why does the Air Force need expensive new bombers? Have the people we've been bombing over the years been complaining?

☎ .... **George Wallace**

Men are brave enough to go to war, but they are not brave enough to get a bikini wax.

☎ .... **Rita Rudner**

Women should be running war. We work out our anger by saying nasty things about the lives of the people we're mad at. We're experts at *biographical* warfare.

☎ .... **Caryn Leschen**

The Pentagon's missile defense system test failed, which makes our military secrets safe. Now the spies have no interest in stealing them.

☎ .... **Bill Maher**

The Marine Corps is studying Wal-Mart's distribution network to help improve their ability to keep supplies flowing in the field. They've also got their cooks studying 7-Eleven to figure out how to get people to eat food that has been sitting on the shelf for three years.

☎ . . . . **Jay Leno**

China sent a message to George W. Bush, that U.S. missile defense proposals will have "a formidable adverse global impact and they're poisoning the trend of multipolarity." In response, George W. Bush said, "What?"

☎ . . . . **Conan O'Brien**

Switzerland is well known for its vicious unrelenting neutrality. That its army is dismantling its bicycle troops is a surprise to those who didn't know Switzerland had an army. There are only a few bicycle troops, but they sound like a lot more when they fix playing cards to rub against the spokes. And the bicycle troops are twice as effective as the unicycle troops.

☎ . . . . **Jon Stewart**

You know what I never understood was the VFW halls. Veterans of Foreign Wars, is the foreign part really necessary? Is there still some Civil War veteran trying to sneak in?

☎ . . . . **Jay Leno**

I'd like to see gays in the military. If my wife will give me a night off now and then.

☎ . . . . Dylan Brody

Twelve hundred women a year are getting pregnant at Fort Polk. That's why they call it Fort Polk. And that's why they call them drill sergeants.

☎ . . . . Bill Maher

I just got out of the service. Postal. Saw a lot of action, though, mostly little dogs. Nothing I couldn't handle with the mace and the kick boxing.

☎ . . . . Margaret Smith

Mimes

My uncle was thrown out of a mime show for having a seizure. They thought he was heckling.

☎ . . . . Jeff Shaw

Money

Misers aren't fun to live with, but they make wonderful ancestors.

☎ . . . . David Brenner

When I was a kid we made money by going to the houses of people who hadn't shoveled their snow, slipping, and suing them.

☎ . . . . Bill Braudis

Money is better than poverty, if only for financial reasons.

☎ . . . . **Woody Allen**

I've got all the money I'll ever need, if I die by four o'clock this afternoon.

☎ . . . . **Henny Youngman**

A bank is a place that will lend you money, if you can prove that you don't need it.

☎ . . . . **Bob Hope**

If you want to know what God thinks of money, just look at the people He gave it to.

☎ . . . . **Dorothy Parker**

Money won't buy friends, but you get a better class of enemy.

☎ . . . . **Spike Milligan**

Someday I want to be rich. Some people get so rich they lose all respect for humanity. That's how rich I want to be.

☎ . . . . **Rita Rudner**

They have ATMs in jails now so criminals can arrange bail money. Do you think they look around when they're using them, looking for shady characters?

☎ . . . . **Jay Leno**

If you had a penny and threw it off the Empire State Building and it hit somebody in the head, it would kill him. Talk about getting your money's worth.

☎ . . . . **Heywood Banks**

Monsters

Of all the monsters, the Wolf Man had it the worst. More body hair than Ed Asner in a lint trap, never able to have a white couch in his house.

☎ . . . . **Dennis Miller**

Mothers

I'm very loyal in a relationship, all relationships. When I'm with my mother, I don't look at other moms, "Wow. I wonder what her macaroni and cheese tastes like."

☎ . . . . **Garry Shandling**

I asked my mother if I was adopted. She said, "Not yet, but we placed an ad."

☎ . . . . **Dana Snow**

My mother never saw the irony in calling me a son-of-a-bitch.

☎ . . . . **Richard Jeni**

My mother is so neurotic, she used to hear voices in her head. Not anymore. Even they don't want to get trapped in a conversation with her.

☎ . . . . **Kate Mason**

Saw my mom today. It was all right, she didn't see me.

☎ . . . . **Margaret Smith**

Movies

A Bug's Life continues to sell well in video. In fact, it's so popular, Motel 6 is now advertising, "Movie stars right in your room!"

☎ .... **Jay Leno**

The movie *Dude, Where's My Car?* did so well, they're working on the sequel: *Oh, There It Is.*

☎ .... **Jon Stewart**

Crouching Tiger, Hidden Dragon sounds like something Siegfried and Roy would do on vacation. I saw the movie and realized I saw no tigers or dragons, but of course they were crouching and hidden.

☎ .... **Steve Martin**

The Exorcist was a landmark movie: both scary and disturbing. It was also the first and last time a Catholic priest actually *wanted* to give a woman control over her own body.

☎ .... **Dennis Miller**

It's the fortieth anniversary of *Psycho,* which has been banned in France for fear it might lead to copycat showers.

☎ .... **Craig Kilborn**

They're talking about upscale movie palaces with gourmet food. "More ground pepper on your Raisinettes?"

☎ .... **Jay Leno**

I was watching a World War Two movie, and I noticed that the Nazis in those movies had a regular "Heil," and then, when they were around the offices, they had this casual "Heil," "Yeah, heil, how are you? Is the kid back with the coffee yet? Yeah, world domination, Aryan race, whose donuts are those? Yeah, heil, nice to see you. Mind if I take the last jelly?"

☎ . . . . **Jerry Seinfeld**

I'll never understand why people go to movie theaters to have conversations. Going to the movies to talk is like going to a restaurant to cook. The idea is that you have paid your money to have someone do something better than you can do it yourself.

☎ . . . . **Rita Rudner**

Music

Nothing separates the generations more than music. By the time a child is eight or nine, he has developed a passion for his own music that is even stronger than his passions for procrastination and weird clothes.

☎ . . . . **Bill Cosby**

Men who listen to classical music tend not to spit.

☎ . . . . **Rita Rudner**

The country music people adopted the slogan: "It's country. Admit it. You love it." Here is one of the rejected slogans: "One banjo. Two chords. Three teeth."

☎ . . . . **Jay Leno**

Jazz is five guys playing different songs. And rap? They left the "c" off the front of that word.

☎ . . . . **Steve McGrew**

I worry that the person who thought up Muzak may be thinking up something else.

☎ . . . . **Lily Tomlin**

MTV Europe is just like MTV in America, except they play videos.

☎ . . . . **Craig Kilborn**

I wrote a song, but I can't read music, so I don't know what it is. Every once in a while I'll be listening to the radio and I say, "I think I might have written that."

☎ . . . . **Steven Wright**

A big company is thinking of buying Napster, and the nineteen-year-old kid who owns it could make one hundred million dollars. Why pay him? Why not just download it for free when the kid's not looking. It's not stealing, it's sharing.

☎ . . . . **Jay Leno**

Napster claims most users just sample the music before buying the album. Yeah, the way college students "sample" Oreos in supermarkets.

☎ . . . . **Jon Stewart**

Seattle's new Rock & Roll Museum was inspired by Jimi Hendrix. The first patron to choke on his own vomit gets a free syringe.

☎ . . . . **Craig Kilborn**

The song "If I Had a Hammer" is geared toward people who don't have a hammer. Maybe before I had a hammer I thought I'd hammer in the morning and hammer in the evening. But once you get a hammer, you find you don't really hammer as much as you thought you would.

☎ . . . . **Ellen DeGeneres**

Talking about music is like dancing about architecture.

☎ . . . . **Steve Martin**

When you are about thirty-five years old, something terrible always happens to music.

☎ . . . . **Steve Race**

Musical Instruments

I play the harmonica. The only way I can play is if I get my car going really fast, and stick it out the window.

☎ . . . . **Steven Wright**

Musicians

When Christina Aguilera was being interviewed just before the Grammys, she said, "I am accustomed to all the 'hecticity' of these events." In a related story, it turns out that Aguilera was the main speechwriter for George W. Bush.

☎ . . . . **Conan O'Brien**

At the Backstreet Boys concerts in Japan the girls screamed so loud the Boys couldn't hear themselves suck.

☎ . . . . **Craig Kilborn**

An analysis of Beethoven's hair shows he suffered from acute lead poisoning. How bad was his HMO, when he had to wait hundreds of years for the lab results? Today a musician with lead in him is a rap star.

☎ . . . . **Jay Leno**

Critics have complained that Billy Joel is so derivative, he even ripped off his motorcycle accident from Bob Dylan.

☎ . . . . **Jon Stewart**

How come so many great blues singers were blind? Didn't they suffer from any other affliction? You never hear about Severely Constipated Lemon Jefferson, with his own unique version of *Moanin' at Midnight*.

☎ . . . . **Danny Liebert**

Jermaine Jackson announced that he wouldn't be showing up for the Jackson 5 reunion because he thought his brother Michael is charging too much for tickets. After hearing about it, Michael Jackson said that to keep peace in the family he would buy Jermaine a ticket.

☎ . . . . **Conan O'Brien**

Mick Jagger turned fifty-seven. He's halfway between being a Stone and passing one.

☎ . . . . **Jay Leno**

Paul McCartney has built a Beatles Web site that's expected to set new records for the number of hits. In a related story, Ringo Starr has gotten his electricity turned back on by claiming he's in an iron lung.

☎ . . . . **Craig Kilborn**

Rapper C-Murder has been arrested and charged with murder in New Orleans. He is now hoping to get a plea bargain to get his name changed to C-Manslaughter.

☎ . . . . **Jay Leno**

One of the members of Mötley Crue is getting divorced. He wants to start blacking out with other women.

☎ . . . . **Craig Kilborn**

One of the members of Rage Against the Machine has quit. He's toning it down in a new group, Annoyance at the Appliances.

☎ . . . . **Jay Leno**

Wayne Newton has officially replaced Bob Hope as the head of the USO to entertain troops overseas. Army generals say the biggest threat to Newton is friendly fire. When told Newton would be performing, American soldiers called it "our biggest setback so far."

☎ . . . . **Jimmy Fallon**

Yanni has come out with a new CD. Just when you thought it was safe to go back in the elevator.

☎ . . . . **Jay Leno**

I love how religious musicians get when they win a Grammy, "I want to thank God for making my song 'Slap That Bitch up Side of the Head' number one!" You think God's pulling for Marilyn Manson's "Burn in Hell"?

☎ .... **Jay Leno**

Keith Richards doesn't strike me as a morning person.

☎ .... **Tom Ryan**

The Rolling Stones have canceled another tour because of health problems. The Rolling Stones are like your grandparents: If you want to see them, you have to go to their house.

☎ .... **Jay Leno**

Mustaches

I love a man with a mustache. And fortunately for me, I've found a man who loves a woman with one.

☎ .... **Aurora Cotsbeck**

Neighborhoods

I live in the barrio. Which, of course, is a Spanish word for ice cream truck.

☎ .... **Brian Dowell**

I hate small towns because once you've seen the cannon in the park there's nothing else to do.

☎ .... **Lenny Bruce**

Greeting cards are specialized now. In rich neighborhoods, cards read, "Sorry I missed your birthday, but you were overseas on business." In my neighborhood the cards read, "Sorry I missed your birthday, but you were in jail. I turned you in because the reward was too big to pass up."

☎ . . . . **Robert Murray**

Suburbia is where the developer bulldozes out the trees, then names the streets after them.

☎ . . . . **Bill Vaughan**

Neighbors

My neighbor asked if he could use my lawnmower, and I told him of course he could, so long as he didn't take it out of my garden.

☎ . . . . **Eric Morecambe**

Neuroses

I'm paranoid about everything. At birth I turned around and looked over my shoulder as I came out of the womb. I thought maybe someone was following me.

☎ . . . . **Richard Lewis**

News

Disneyland celebrated its fortieth anniversary by burying a time capsule. They say it will be dug up in fifty years, or when the last person in line at Space Mountain gets to the front, whichever comes first.

☎ . . . . **Jay Leno**

On the fiftieth anniversary of V-J Day, the victory over Japan, New York had a huge celebration in Times Square. There must have been ten thousand people right between the big Mitsubishi billboard and the jumbo Sonytron.

☎ . . . . **David Letterman**

I'm very much against the news: "Here are eleven more things to upset you. Film at eleven."

☎ . . . . **Eric Idle**

President Bush announced today that they have stopped a terrorist organization that has taken millions and millions away from the American people. Yes, the IRS is finished!

☎ . . . . **Jay Leno**

Newspapers

It's amazing that the amount of news that happens in the world every day always just exactly fits the newspaper.

☎ . . . . **Jerry Seinfeld**

Dear Abby: 98 percent of the people who write her get a letter, "Stop bothering me, you whiny sack of manure."

☎ . . . . **David Letterman**

New York

Welcome to New York, where every tourist is a walking ATM machine.

☎ . . . . **David Letterman**

In yet another effort to clean up New York City, the mayor urged the city council to pass legislation that would require alternate side of the street urination.

☎ . . . . **Dennis Miller**

People say New Yorkers can't get along. Not true. I saw two New Yorkers, complete strangers, sharing a cab. One guy took the tires and the radio; the other guy took the engine.

☎ . . . . **David Letterman**

The new mayor, Michael Bloomberg, says that he intends on taking the subway to work every day. He also says he plans on showing up late and smelling like urine.

☎ . . . . **Conan O'Brien**

New York now has two hundred new portable toilets. They're yellow, have four wheels and a driver with a weird name.

☎ . . . . **David Letterman**

It's nice to work in New York City in the fall. It's nice to walk down Madison Avenue and see the trees turning from charcoal gray to charcoal brown.

☎ . . . . **Joe E. Lewis**

The Statue of Liberty's crown has been declared a fire hazard, so tourists will be confined to her ass. Her head could burst into flames. They had the same problem with Don King.

☎ . . . . **David Letterman**

A new report says that most New York cabs are really noisy and have lumpy seats. Coincidentally, the same goes for their drivers.

☎ . . . . **Conan O'Brien**

Someone did a study of the three most-often-heard phrases in New York City. One is, "Hey, taxi!" Two is, "What train do I take to get to Bloomingdales?" And three is, "Don't worry, it's only a flesh wound."

☎ . . . . **David Letterman**

New York's such a wonderful city. Although I was at the library today. The guys are very rude. I said, "I'd like a card." He says, "You have to prove you're a citizen of New York." So I stabbed him.

☎ . . . . **Emo Philips**

Nobel Prize

I read that the Nobel Prize is getting a little crowded with nominees and new categories. If they really want to narrow the field, they should add a swimsuit competition.

☎ . . . . **Danny Liebert**

Two Americans have won the Nobel Prize in economics. They're the first to figure out all the little charges on their phone bill.

☎ . . . . **Jay Leno**

Nuclear

The Chernobyl nuclear plant has finally been closed. *Chernobyl* is the Russian word for Amtrak.

☎ . . . . **Craig Kilborn**

Nude Beaches

People in X-rated movies have been screened by a casting director. That doesn't happen in real life. A nude beach isn't like the Playboy Channel. It's more like the Discovery Channel.

☎ . . . . **Tim Young**

I bought a house on the beach. I thought it was a nude beach, but it turned out to be a giggle beach. When I appeared, everybody giggled.

☎ . . . . **Adam Sandler**

I'm very insecure. I get depressed when I find out that the people I hate don't like me. I'm kind of paranoid, too. I often think the car in front of me is following me the long way around.

☎ . . . . **Dennis Miller**

Olympics

Our new Olympic uniforms have just been unveiled, and they prove one thing: America is a nation of sluts.

☎ . . . . **Craig Kilborn**

The female hockey team won in the Olympics. Forty women with sticks and missing teeth. More commonly called Kentucky.

☎ . . . . **Jay Leno**

Luge strategy? Lie flat and try not to die.

☎ . . . . **Tim Steeves**

Women like curling. They get to see men pushing brooms.

☎ . . . . **Jay Leno**

Black folks are good at the Olympic sports you can learn to do free in the park. The white guy in track knows he's coming in last. He's just running for the jacket.

☎ . . . . **D. L. Hughley**

The original Olympics were all held in the nude. That sure changed men's hurdles. The white guys won a lot more races.

☎ . . . . **Tim Young**

A lot of people are upset at the extent of the Olympic drug testing. I guess it depends on whether you see the urine cup as half full or half empty.

☎ . . . . **Jay Leno**

I went to the Olympics, but I could only get tickets for synchronized swimming. I hate to say this, but I prayed for one of them to get a cramp because, if I understand the rules correctly, if one of them drowns, they all have to.

☎ . . . . **Anthony Clark**

If they're making bowling an Olympic sport, why not drinking and driving, or waking up next to a fat girl?

☎ . . . . **Dave Attell**

Chess will be accepted as an Olympic sport in the 2006 games. The other Olympic athletes are excited that the chess players are joining them, and say they're looking forward to giving them wedgies and taking their lunch money.

☎ . . . . **Conan O'Brien**

My wife wants Olympic sex, once every four years.

☎ . . . . . **Rodney Dangerfield**

Operations

I had general anesthesia. That's so weird. You go to sleep in one room, and then you wake up four hours later in a totally different room. Just like college.

☎ . . . . **Ross Shafer**

Opportunity

Don't be afraid of missing opportunities. Behind every failure is an opportunity somebody wishes they had missed.

☎ . . . . Lily Tomlin

Outdoors

I hate the outdoors. To me the outdoors is where the car is.

☎ . . . . Will Durst

I was walking along the ocean. That's generally where you'll find the beach. Looking for ashtrays in their wild state.

☎ . . . . Ronnie Graham

I was walking in a forest, and a tree fell right in front of me and Keebler elves went everywhere.

☎ . . . . Buzz Nutley

Parenting

Why do you need a license for driving, hunting, and fishing, yet when it comes to parenting all you need to get started is a bottle of Cuervo and a pinball machine?

☎ . . . . Jeff Shaw

Parents should conduct their arguments in quiet, respectful tones, but in a foreign language. You'd be surprised what an inducement that is to the education of children.

☎ . . . . Judith Martin

Parents are not quite interested in injustice, they are interested in quiet.

☎ .... **Bill Cosby**

I don't think my parents liked me. They put a live teddy bear in my crib.

☎ .... **Woody Allen**

My childhood should have taught me lessons for my own parenthood, but it didn't because parenting can be learned only by people who have no children.

☎ .... **Bill Cosby**

We are all born charming, fresh, and spontaneous, and must be civilized before we are fit to participate in society.

☎ .... **Judith Martin**

Parties

I once went to a costume party wearing boxer shorts. I have terrible varicose veins, so I went as a road map.

☎ .... **Woody Allen**

Perfume

Scientists say sniffing perfume can improve your memory. Do you believe that? Those models in Calvin Klein's Obsession ads can't even remember which sex they are.

☎ .... **Jay Leno**

I love watching women put on their perfume. They always hit the inside of the wrist. Women are convinced that this is the most action-packed area. Why? In case you slap the guy, he still finds you intriguing? CRACK! "Oh … *Chanel*."

☎ . . . . **Jerry Seinfeld**

Pets

I bought an ant farm. I don't know where I'm gonna find a tractor that small.

☎ . . . . **Steven Wright**

My brother had a hamster. He took it to see the vet; that's like bringing a disposable lighter for repair.

☎ . . . . **Wayne Cotter**

No one can feel as helpless as the owner of a sick goldfish.

☎ . . . . **Kin Hubbard**

Ever let your parakeet out of its cage? My parakeet will fly across the room, right into the mirror … He will hit that mirror: *bang!* He's so stupid. Even if he thought the mirror was another room, you'd think he'd try to avoid hitting the other parakeet.

☎ . . . . **Jerry Seinfeld**

Philosophy

I have an existential map. It has "You are here" written all over it.

☎ . . . . **Steven Wright**

Nietzsche says that we will live the same life, over and over again. God, I'll have to sit through the Ice Capades again.

☎ . . . . **Woody Allen**

I was once walking through the forest alone. A tree fell right in front of me, and I didn't hear it.

☎ . . . . **Steven Wright**

Every once in a while I feel that I am at two with the universe.

☎ . . . . **Woody Allen**

If a college student is looking for a degree in philosophy, Starbucks is opening six hundred more stores.

☎ . . . . **Jay Leno**

I majored in philosophy and landed a job as a morning DJ on all-philosophy radio station WYMI. "Good morning, it's 8:05. For those of you who are just waking up: What's the point?"

☎ . . . . **Mike Dugan**

Physique

Feeling shitty about your physique is an important state of mind, for it leads one into a series of diverse, unfulfilling relationships. As opposed to just one monogamous journey into the banal.

☎ . . . . **Janeane Garofalo**

I sacrificed my body to the goddess of motherhood. I used to have a waist. I'm still keeping the pants because they fit around my head now.

☎ .... **Stephanie Hodge**

I read an article that said in American society fat people are looked down upon because they are considered sloppy and disorganized, so they don't get promoted at work. American fat people, come to Japan, you'll get some respect. You can say, "I'm an aspiring sumo wrestler." And the Japanese people will say, "Go ahead! Super-size that tempura, fat ass!"

☎ .... **Naoko Okamoto**

I hate skinny women, because no matter how thin, they're still always on a diet. My friend Cynthia is 5'9" and 102 pounds, has been on Phen Fen, Metabolife, and lives on Slim Fast. Used to be she'd ask, "Do I look fat in this?" Now she says, "Can you still see me? Am I still visible to the naked eye?"

☎ .... **Kelly Maguire**

I got kind of thick around the waist here. I got one of those shirts with snaps on the bottom. Shoot, those snaps haven't seen each other since they left Macy's.

☎ .... **Roz Browne**

Picnics

My girlfriend and I went on a picnic. I don't know how she did it, but she got poison ivy on the brain. When it itched, the only way she could scratch it was to think about sandpaper.

☎ . . . . **Steven Wright**

Piercings

I'm trying to look both hip and thin, so I got my lips pierced, and had 'em clipped together with a big gold stud.

☎ . . . . **Caryn Leschen**

Poison

My cousin accidentally swallowed some poison. So to induce vomiting, we gave him a beer and rushed him right to the nearest college fraternity.

☎ . . . . **Wally Wang**

Police

A recent police study found that you're much more likely to get shot by a fat cop if you run.

☎ . . . . **Dennis Miller**

The Miranda ruling has been upheld. But when a cop is sticking a plunger up your ass, it's hard to remain silent.

☎ . . . . **Bill Maher**

Lawyer Alan Dershowitz says that police are routinely trained to lie. That's the difference between lawyers and police. Police are trained to lie, but lying comes naturally to lawyers.

☎ .... **Jay Leno**

Police in Washington, D.C., are now using cameras to catch drivers who go through red lights. Many congressmen this week opposed the use of the red light cameras incorrectly assuming they were being used for surveillance at local brothels.

☎ .... **Dennis Miller**

Political Correctness

It's a new era at Disney. From now on, Snow White and the Seven Dwarfs will be known as Person of No Color and the Seven Vertically Challenged Individuals.

☎ .... **Argus Hamilton**

Politics

The Democrats are the party that says government will make you smarter, taller, richer, and remove the crabgrass on your lawn. The Republicans are the party that says government doesn't work, and then they get elected and prove it.

☎ .... **P. J. O'Rourke**

On Capitol Hill, Republicans announced plans for a national museum honoring African Americans. The Republicans say the only thing holding the project up is finding a location that's not in their neighborhood.

☎ .... **Conan O'Brien**

The number of Americans living in poverty has dropped recently, and Republicans are attributing it to proposed cuts in welfare. And they hope that by cutting Medicare, they'll also be able to reduce the number of the elderly.

☎ .... **Johnny Robish**

State legislators are merely politicians whose darkest secret prohibits them from running for higher office.

☎ .... **Dennis Miller**

Assuming that either the left wing or the right wing gained control of the country, it would probably fly around in circles.

☎ .... **Pat Paulsen**

There's something about Marxism that brings out warts, the only kind of growth this economic system encourages.

☎ .... **P. J. O'Rourke**

My kid is a conservative. "Why is that?" you ask. Remember in the sixties, when we told you if you kept using drugs your kids would be mutants?

☎ .... **Mort Sahl**

Pat Buchanan says there's no room in his party for racists and bigots. They're full up. Apply next year.

☎ .... **Jay Leno**

Whatever happened to separation of church and hate? It's amazing how, in an election year, God's name gets thrown around like a drunken dwarf at a biker rally.

☎ .... **Dennis Miller**

Now I know what a statesman is; he's a dead politician. We need more statesmen.

☎ .... **Bill Vaughan**

Pornography

Pin-up pictures from *Playboy* will be available to download to mobile phones soon. And you thought simply talking on the phone at the dinner table was a problem.

☎ .... **Jon Stewart**

I saw a blind man rent a porno video. He must really like bad music.

☎ .... **Mark Gross**

I had to learn sex from porno movies. That doesn't work. Learning sex from porno, that's like learning how to drive by watching the Indianapolis 500.

☎ .... **Norman K.**

Postage

A word of warning to postal customers. Don't lick the new Jerry Garcia stamp.

☎ . . . . **Jay Leno**

Pregnancy

My period was late, and I had nothing to worry about, but I worried anyway: "Maybe I *am* going to have the Lord's child."

☎ . . . . . . **Penelope Lombard**

Doctor says to a man, "You're pregnant." The man asks, "How does a man get pregnant?" The doctor says, "The usual way: a little wine, a little dinner . . ."

☎ . . . . **Henny Youngman**

I know lots of women who have had children. But I'm not sure it's for me. "Feel the baby kicking, feel the baby kicking," says my friend who is deliriously happy about it. To me, life is tough enough without having someone kick you from the inside.

☎ . . . . **Rita Rudner**

When I was growing up, the fertility drug was alcohol.

☎ . . . . **Kelly Monteith**

You should never say anything to a woman that even remotely suggests that you think she's pregnant unless you can see an actual baby emerging from her at that moment.

☎ . . . . **Dave Barry**

The University of Edinburgh has found a way for men to get other men pregnant. A guy wouldn't say he had a bun in the oven. What would it be, a keg in the cooler? And now we could be seeing Siegfried and Roy and Son.

☎ .... Jay Leno

Premenstrual Syndrome

Women complain about PMS, but I think of it as the only time of the month when I can be myself.

☎ .... Roseanne

Doctors are prescribing Prozac for women with severe PMS. Not in pill form. The husband shoots it into her from fifty feet away with a dart gun.

☎ .... Jay Leno

PMS is this very difficult hormonal syndrome that causes women, for four or five days out of every month, to behave exactly the way men do all the time.

☎ .... Dylan Brody

Science has found that men may suffer from PMS. Men suffer, too. The saddest part? I have my mother's thighs.

☎ .... Craig Kilborn

Presidents

So how do I pick a president? Much the same way I choose a driver to the airport. Which one will cost me the least, and not get me killed.

☎ . . . . **Dennis Miller**

Here's the George W. Bush quote of the day:"More and more of our imports are coming from overseas." Right. Like 100 percent.

☎ . . . . **Jay Leno**

We need a president who's fluent in at least one language.

☎ . . . . **Buck Henry**

The vice presidency is sort of like the last cookie on the plate. Everybody insists he won't take it, but somebody always does.

☎ . . . . **Bill Vaughan**

All the old sexist arguments against a woman president have been shot down by, ironically, men. Women are ruled by their biology? For chrissakes, a red-assed monkey masturbating at the zoo is in more control of his impulses than three-quarters of Congress. Women are too shallow, too concerned with frilly fashions and feminine makeup? Yes, I suppose those are traits best left out of the Oval Office, because they're much more suited to the head of the FBI.

☎ . . . . **Dennis Miller**

People say satire is dead. It's not dead; it's alive and living in the White House.

☎ .... **Robin Williams**

Protests

The main accomplishment of almost all organized protests is to annoy people who are not in them.

☎ .... **Dave Barry**

Pat Buchanan says the Native Americans protesting Columbus Day should just go back where they came from.

☎ .... **Conan O'Brien**

Psychics

If it's the Psychic Network why do they need a phone number?

☎ .... **Robin Williams**

A psychic woman claims to be able to tell a man's future by having sex with him. Can't every woman do this? You have sex, and the man falls asleep.

☎ .... **Craig Kilborn**

My mother thinks she's psychic. My whole life, my sisters and I have gone along with it, but I don't know how much longer I can keep up the charade. This week it's my turn to have an accident.

☎ .... **Margaret Smith**

Racing

I went to see a NASCAR race. Where did they get the name? Did two guys in North Carolina try to impress each other? "Hey Bubba, look at mah new Chevrolet.""WHOOOEEEE, *nahhhhhsssss car.*"

☎ . . . . **Dobie Maxwell**

Horse sense is the thing a horse has which keeps it from betting on people.

☎ . . . . **W. C. Fields**

Some people play a horse to win, some to place. I should have bet this horse to live.

☎ . . . . **Henny Youngman**

The Kentucky Derby is for horses that are only three years old. Or as the Sizzler calls them, veal.

☎ . . . . **Jay Leno**

Radio

I am amazed at radio DJs today. I am firmly convinced that AM on my radio stands for Absolute Moron. I will not begin to tell you what FM stands for.

☎ . . . . **Jasper Carrott**

Real Estate

I sold my house this week. I got a pretty good price for it, but it made my landlord mad as hell.

☎ . . . . **Garry Shandling**

We just bought a house. My husband calls it a "fixer-upper." I call it a piece of crap.

☎ .... **Maryellen Hooper**

Reality

Reality is the leading cause of stress amongst those in touch with it.

☎ .... **Lily Tomlin**

Rednecks

You might be a redneck: if you mow your lawn and find a car, if your honeymoon was featured on *True Stories of the Highway Patrol*, or if you name your children after the cars in which they were conceived.

☎ .... **Jeff Foxworthy**

I come from what I think of as *borderline* white trash. Meaning, none of us have ever married a cousin, just in-laws.

☎ .... **Andi Rhoads**

Relationships

Relationships are great in the beginning: You call each other by those cute little pet names. My last boyfriend used to call me "Honey Lamb," and I'd call him "Satan." We eventually grew apart. On weekends, I'd want to go antiquing, and he'd want to round up minions and take over the world.

☎ .... **Kelly Maguire**

Men and women just look at life completely different. Women are playing chess, we plan relationships ten moves ahead. Meanwhile, the guy is playing checkers, thinking just one move ahead, "Jump me!"

☎ . . . . **Margot Black**

Honesty is the key to a relationship. If you can fake that, you're in.

☎ . . . . **Richard Jeni**

Relationships are a lot like drugs. You develop a dependency, and if you're not really careful you could wind up losing your house.

☎ . . . . **Mike Dugan**

I hate all those books on how to find the perfect relationship. No book can tell you that. But I could write one on ending relationships, *How to Be a Psycho Bitch*. Featuring chapters like: "The Art of Slashing Tires" and "How to Scare Off the New Girlfriend by Describing His Little Weenie."

☎ . . . . . . **Christine O'Rourke**

Religion

To you I'm an atheist; to God, I'm the Loyal Opposition.

☎ . . . . **Woody Allen**

Born again? No, I'm not. Excuse me for getting it right the first time.

☎ . . . . **Dennis Miller**

I was recently born again.
I must admit it's a glorious
and wonderful experience.
I can't say my mother
enjoyed it a whole lot.

☎ . . . . **John Wing**

An image of the Virgin Mary
has appeared in smudges on
a window in Perth Amboy,
New Jersey. Rejoice, oh ye of
little Windex.

☎ . . . . **Jon Stewart**

Was the Buddha married?
His wife would say, "Are
you just going to sit
around like that all day?"

☎ **Garry Shandling**

We were skeptical Catholics.
We believed Jesus walked
on water. We just figured it
was probably winter.

☎ . . . . **John Wing**

When I was a kid my mother
switched religions from
Catholic to Episcopalian.
Which is what, Catholic Lite?
One-third less guilt than
regular religion.

☎ . . . . **Rick Corso**

Do you realize that of all the
major religions, Christianity
is the only one that has a
messiah and that it is also
the only one that allows the
unrestricted eating of pork?
As Christians, not only do we
believe we have the only
God, he also eats bacon.

☎ . . . . **Chris Bliss**

I'm Catholic, and my mother said we were born to suffer. So I married an attorney.

☎ .... **Maura Kennedy**

The story of Adam and Eve made no sense to me. Eve is responsible for the entire decline of humanity because she was tempted by an apple. Don't you think God over-reacted just a tad? It's not like Eve ate God's last Oreo.

☎ .... **Margot Black**

Gentiles are people who eat mayonnaise for no reason.

☎ .... **Robin Williams**

Either heaven or hell will have continuous background music. Which one you think it will be tells a lot about you.

☎ .... **Bill Vaughan**

Billy Graham has described heaven as a family reunion that never ends. What must hell be like? Home videos of the same reunion.

☎ .... **Barry Steiger**

Most major religions use hell as a deterrent to bad activity. But I find the concept of hell quite comforting because, hey, at least I'll know people there.

☎ .... **Margot Black**

Maybe there is no actual place called hell. Maybe hell is just having to listen to our grandparents breathe through their noses when they're eating sandwiches.

☎ .... **Jim Carrey**

What if all the religions were represented at the pearly gates? We might hear the following: "I just wanted to let everyone know: Baptists, Catholics, Muslims, Buddhists, Agnostics, Atheists, you were way off. Rastafarians, follow me. And bring your lighters."

☎ .... **Tom Ryan**

The bible says Jesus has skin of brass. But they did not have to describe Jesus for me to know that he was black. I could tell by the miracles he did. Jesus' first miracle was turning water into wine at a wedding. "Lord, we done ran out of wine!" "Normally I don't do this, but y'all go on, keep the party goin'." "*Go Jesus! Go Jesus!*"

☎ .... **D. L. Hughley**

In the movies, Jesus is always played by someone who looks like Ted Nugent. You never have a Jewish Jesus, "I've got lepers here, you bastards. I walked across water, you can come and open the damn door."

☎ .... **Robin Williams**

Hey, doncha think the real reason Jesus Christ hasn't returned is those crosses you wear? How would JFK feel if you wore little rifles on your lapels?

☎ .... **Bill Hicks**

Do you know what you get when you cross a Jehovah's Witness with an Atheist? Someone who knocks on your door for no apparent reason.

☎ .... **Guy Owen**

I'm Jewish, but those Hasidic Jews, the guys with the hats and beards, make me feel guilty. They've got a personal relationship with God. Me, I'm not sure God exists. These guys not only talk directly to God, He picks their wardrobe.

☎ . . . . **Norman K.**

I'm very adaptable, I can fit into any group. Last weekend I joined this religious cult, now I'm in charge of the Nikes and Kool-Aid.

☎ . . . . **Fran Chernowsky**

Dial-a-Prayer hung up on me.

☎ . . . . **Jackie Vernon**

We were Pentecostal. That's just a light bulb and a car away from being Amish.

☎ . . . . **Renee Hicks**

The Pope's new Fiat, which can withstand direct machine-gun fire, was actually designed for John Tesh. The Pope will use the $1.3 million car to fulfill one of his duties, waving at the poor.

☎ . . . . **Craig Kilborn**

The Pope is on a goodwill tour of the Middle East. Who better to settle problems between Muslims and Jews than someone who's had experience persecuting both?

☎ . . . . **Jon Stewart**

The Pope apologized for everything his posse has done over the last two thousand years: "Hey, dudes, it was nothing personal."

☎ . . . . **Craig Kilborn**

I admire the Pope. I have a lot of respect for anyone who can tour without an album.

☎ .... **Rita Rudner**

When I was growing up my mother wanted me to be a priest, but I think it's a tough occupation. Can you imagine giving up your sex life and once a week people come in and tell you all the highlights of theirs?

☎ .... **Tom Dreesen**

The Torah has something to say about teenagers: According to one of the commentators, the reason that Abraham was about to sacrifice Isaac at the age of twelve and not thirteen, is because at thirteen it wouldn't have been a sacrifice.

☎ .... **Bob Alper**

I saw this guy at the baseball game all year, holding up a sign: "John 13." I looked it up. It said, "Go, Mookie!"

☎ .... **Alan Havey**

The Religious Right is really getting out of control. Today they were at the grocery store blocking the home pregnancy test aisle.

☎ .... **Melissa Maroff**

The Dalai Lama met with Senator Jesse Helms in D.C. The Dalai Lama had to start out slow with Jesse: "All right, what's the sound of two hands clapping?"

☎ .... **Jon Stewart**

I was walking across a bridge one day, and I saw a man standing on the edge, about to jump off. So I ran over and said, "Stop! don't do it! There's so much to live for!" He said, "Like what?" I said, "Well, are you religious or atheist?" "Religious." I said, "Me too! Are you Christian or Buddhist?" "Christian." I said, "Me too! Are you Catholic or Protestant?" "Protestant." I said, "Me too! Are you Episcopalian or Baptist?" "Baptist." I said, "Wow! Me too! Are you Baptist Church of God or Baptist Church of the Lord?" "Baptist Church of God." I said, "Me too! Are you original Baptist Church of God, or are you Reformed Baptist Church of God?" "Reformed Baptist Church of God." I said, "Me too! Are you Reformed Baptist Church of God, Reformation of 1879, or Reformed Baptist Church of God, Reformation of 1915?" He said, "Reformed Baptist Church of God, Reformation of 1915." I said, "Die, heretic scum," and pushed him off.

☎ .... **Emo Philips**

On going to war over religion: You're basically killing each other to see who's got the better imaginary friend.

☎ .... **Richard Jeni**

I've been studying Zen Buddhism. Zen teaches the value of doing and thinking nothing. I thought, "Cool, I was fired for being a zen master."

☎ .... **Dana Snow**

Restaurants

That National Rifle Association theme restaurant in Times Square is offering 10 percent off your steak if you can locate the exit wound. The other special is Chicken on a Deathbed of Rice.

☎ . . . . **David Letterman**

I can't leave a restaurant without leftovers. And they're not always from my plate. "You gonna eat that? Oh yeah? I better get back to my table now." Some restaurants actually get uncomfortable wrapping something up in tin foil, so they disguise it as a swan figurine. I'm like, "You might want to make that swan some babies, because I'm taking these Sweet 'n Low, too."

☎ . . . . **Margaret Smith**

I am originally from Israel The other day at a restaurant in Malibu, I really liked the waiter, who was a very good-looking guy, blond with blue eyes, so I decided to order "Sex on the Beach." Well, in Israel it's free. Hey, nobody told me it was a drink.

☎ . . . . **Irit Noy**

A waitress in Dallas has donated a kidney to one of her regular customers. Now for the rest of his life he's going to have to tip at least 40 percent.

☎ . . . . **Jay Leno**

Last night I ordered an entire meal in French, and even the waiter was surprised. It was a Chinese restaurant.

☎ . . . . **Henny Youngman**

A maître d' at an exclusive restaurant in New York received a sixteen thousand–dollar tip from a Wall Street customer. Unfortunately, this morning the tip was only valued at four thousand dollars.

☎ . . . . **Conan O'Brien**

Roommates

Living with my roommate was like buying a new lamp. They both had three settings: dim, dimmer, dimmest.

☎ . . . . **Joel Warshaw**

I've had six roommates in the last six months. Living with them is like taking out the trash: They all smell, and I throw them out at the end of the week.

☎ . . . . **Pete Zamora**

Royalty

Prince Harry of England has admitted experimenting with marijuana. Hey, Your Highness, that's just an expression.

☎ . . . . **Craig Kilborn**

On her one hundredth birthday, reporters asked the Queen Mum what part of her life she remembered most fondly, and she replied, "Breakfast."

☎ . . . . **Craig Kilborn**

Running

A friend of mine runs marathons. He always talks about this "runner's high," but he has to go twenty-six miles for it. That's why I smoke and drink. I get the same feeling from a flight of stairs.

☎ .... **Larry Miller**

A friend of mine jogs ten miles a day. If you ever catch me running ten miles in a row, tell the bus driver my arm is caught in the door.

☎ .... **Jeff Shaw**

The trouble with jogging is that the ice falls out of your glass.

☎ .... **Martin Mull**

I jogged for three miles once. It was the worst three hours of my life.

☎ .... **Rita Rudner**

I pulled a hamstring during the New York City Marathon. An hour into the race I jumped up off the couch.

☎ .... **David Letterman**

Last year I entered the Los Angeles marathon. I finished last. It was embarrassing. And the guy who was in front of me, second to last, was making fun of me. He said, "How does it feel to come in last?" I said, "You want to know?" So I dropped out.

☎ .... **Gerry Bednob**

I ran three miles today. Finally I said, "Lady, take your purse!"

☎ .... **Emo Philips**

A new study says sex before a marathon is a good thing. Now men can legitimately say, "Sorry, babe, gotta run."

☎ . . . . **Jay Leno**

Ruts

I feel like I'm in a rut. Every time I go to bed at night, I find myself just getting up again in the morning.

☎ . . . . **Brad Stine**

Salaries

In 1914, Henry Ford adopted a minimum wage of five dollars a day for his workers. Today in his honor, Nike agreed, "Okay, we'll match that."

☎ . . . . **Jay Leno**

Satellites

The government has this satellite 250 miles up that takes pictures so accurate, it can identify individual humans on the ground. I don't trust it. This is the same government that takes my picture three feet away and makes me look like a Klingon.

☎ . . . . **Wayne Cotter**

Every so often, I like to go to the window, look up, and smile for a satellite picture.

☎ . . . . **Steven Wright**

School

Nothing I learned in school prepared me for life on any level. My first book should have read, "See Dick balance his checkbook. See Jane leave an unhealthy relationship. Run, Jane, run!"

☎ . . . . **Kate Mason**

In California, some high schools are requiring students to wear uniforms. They say uniforms create a safe, stable environment. You know, like the post office.

☎ . . . . **Jay Leno**

I'm willing to see prayer in our schools, if you're willing to find a place for algebra in our churches.

☎ . . . . **Dylan Brody**

Supporters point to Bush's education record in Texas, where school test scores have actually risen. But did they really rise, or did they just hit bottom so hard that they bounced?

☎ . . . . **Dennis Miller**

Seattle has installed Web cams in the classroom so parents at home can watch their kids have affairs with their teachers.

☎ . . . . **Craig Kilborn**

In a poll, 58 percent of high school students admitted they'd cheated on tests, and 78 percent had cheated on the teachers they were sleeping with.

☎ . . . . **Jay Leno**

In Wisconsin, a teacher tried to show her third-grade class a video about dinosaurs, but the kids ended up seeing a porno tape left in the VCR by a janitor. And now the third graders believe that dinosaurs went extinct because they got it on with a pizza man.

☎ . . . . **Conan O'Brien**

The Bush administration announced they're no longer going to test school lunches for salmonella. They figure the arsenic in the water will kill the germs.

☎ . . . . **Jay Leno**

It's high school prom season here in New York. The hardest part for the kids is how to rent a white tux that doesn't show a holster bulge.

☎ . . . . **David Letterman**

A study shows the average high school prom-goer spends $1,000. Or $1,009, if you count the pregnancy test.

☎ . . . . **Jay Leno**

> *I went to an all-girls school, where I was captain of the virginity team. "Go, go, go. No, no, no."*
>
> ☎ **Caroline Rhea**

In Orange County they are trying a new law to prevent truancy. When kids skip class, the parents can be taken to jail. Is this a good idea? "Hey, let's all go to Billy's house. His parents are in jail!"

☎ . . . . **Jay Leno**

Science

Scientists are trying to create a black hole. If they succeed, the entire galaxy will be sucked into Brookhaven, Long Island.

☎ . . . . **Steve Carell**

Cloning humans is now legal in England. They should learn how to make a decent hamburger first.

☎ . . . . **Jay Leno**

They've mapped the entire human genome. But the bad news is that the audio version will be narrated by William Shatner.

☎ . . . . **Bill Maher**

Scientists have a new theory that if all the light in the universe was collected and mixed together, it would be a turquoise color. This goes to prove a theory of mine, that the universe is gay.

☎ . . . . **Craig Kilborn**

Scientists say they have found water in the sun. There are apparently large areas with moisture drops on the sun. You know what this means? It's not only hot in the sun, there's also that humid heat.

☎ . . . . **Jay Leno**

The scientific theory I like best is that the rings of Saturn are composed entirely of lost airline luggage.

☎ . . . . **Mark Russell**

This whole thing about sending the elderly into space is part of NASA's study to determine if it's possible to hold a Rolling Stones concert in outer space.

☎ .... **Jay Leno**

Scientists successfully transferred the DNA of a jellyfish to a monkey. It's big news in Washington. If it can be done on humans, it will be the first known way to produce spinelessness on demand, without the use of soft money.

☎ .... **Argus Hamilton**

It is impossible to travel faster than the speed of light, and certainly not desirable, as one's hat keeps blowing off.

☎ .... **Woody Allen**

A scientist in Australia has developed biodegradable car parts that are made out of hemp. The only problem is that the car keeps pulling over because it thinks it sees the cops.

☎ .... **Conan O'Brien**

Forty-five million pagers were out of service after the Galaxy 4 satellite system fell out of orbit. See what happens when you make Bill Gates mad?

☎ .... **Jay Leno**

The first child born from a frozen embryo has turned sixteen. She spent the day chillin'.

☎ .... **Jay Leno**

Here's a story about the liquid being removed from cow manure, leaving only solids. The liquid is then sold to Dr Pepper.

☎ .... **David Letterman**

Scientists have successfully transplanted the head of one monkey onto another monkey, and now they want to try it on humans. You'd take someone with a good mind and sick body and transplant his head onto a healthy body. So Dick Cheney said to George W., "How about it?"

☎ .... **Jay Leno**

By 2020, scientists will be able to implant an orgasm chip in the brain. The operation will take about two minutes for a man and much, much longer for a woman.

☎ .... **Conan O'Brien**

Science Fiction

According to a recent study, 10 percent of *Star Trek* fans meet the psychological criteria for addiction. Deprived of their favorite show, some Trekkies display withdrawal symptoms similar to those of drug addicts. Of course, the real difference is that drug addicts aren't nearly as annoying.

☎ .... **Jay Leno**

Star Trek fans are currently embroiled in a bitter controversy. Half of them say they should be called Trekkies, and the other half think they should be called Trekkers. It's probably just as accurate to call them virgins.

☎ . . . . **Wally Wang**

The new high-tech *Star Wars* toys will be in stores any day now. The toys can talk and are interactive, so they can be easily distinguished from *Star Wars* fans.

☎ . . . . **Conan O'Brien**

Seasons

I think we are going to have an early fall. I was walking down the street today and I saw Michael Jackson changing colors right in front of my eyes.

☎ . . . . **Craig Kilborn**

Self-Esteem

I know a guy who has such low self-esteem that he keeps his keys on him when he walks through the airport metal detector, just so he can get some acknowledgment.

☎ . . . . **Daniel Lybra**

You have heard the adage "You can't love another until you can love yourself." I disagree. It may be difficult to enter into a healthy relationship whilst marinating in a quagmire of self-loathing. But it is a mere can of corn to devote twenty-three hours a day to obsessing over someone who is only vaguely aware that you borrowed the Metro section of his newspaper at Starbucks.

☎ . . . . **Janeane Garofalo**

Self-Help

My dad's been listening to these subliminal self-help tapes. He said, "I've never felt better in my life. These are the best tapes in the world. You must buy the whole set. You must buy the whole set." I picked 'em up. I've been listening to them as I go to sleep. And I've got to tell you, I've never felt better in my life. These are the best tapes in the world. You must buy the whole set. You must buy the whole set.

☎ . . . . **Dylan Brody**

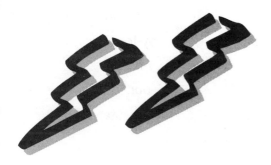

I don't understand motivation books. It's a fairly simple thing: Either you want to do something or you don't; there's no mystery. If you're motivated enough to go to the store and buy a motivation book, aren't you motivated enough to do that? So you don't need the book. Put it back.

☎ . . . . **George Carlin**

Self-Image

Men are self-confident because they grow up identifying with superheroes. Women have bad self-images because they grow up identifying with Barbie.

☎ . . . . **Rita Rudner**

I'm getting very comfortable with my body. I'm sleeping on a full-length mirror.

☎ . . . . **Sandra Bernhard**

Sensitivity

Men are sensitive in strange ways. If a man has built a fire and the last log does not burn, he will take it personally.

☎ . . . . **Rita Rudner**

7-Eleven

I went to a 7-Eleven and asked for a two-by-four and a box of three-by-fives. The clerk said, "Ten-four."

☎ . . . . **Steven Wright**

If mini-marts are open 365 days a year, twenty-four hours a day, and seven days a week, why do the doors have locks on them?

☎ . . . . **Gallagher**

Sex

The human race has been set up. Someone, somewhere, is playing a practical joke on us. Apparently, women need to feel loved to have sex. Men need to have sex to feel loved. How do we ever get started?

☎ . . . . **Billy Connolly**

Don't have sex, man. It leads to kissing, and pretty soon you have to start talking to them.

☎ . . . . **Steve Martin**

Lead us not into temptation. Just tell us where it is; we'll find it.

☎ . . . . **Sam Levenson**

Women might be able to fake orgasms. But men can fake whole relationships.

☎ . . . . **Jimmy Shubert**

I can't express my sexual need, except to strangers over the phone. Then I can go for hours, even through that loud whistle.

☎ . . . . **Garry Shandling**

I read in *Cosmopolitan* that women like to have whipped cream sprayed on their breasts. Unfortunately, my girlfriend has silicone implants. So I use nondairy topping.

☎ . . . . **Jeff Shaw**

Men reach their sexual peak at eighteen. Women reach theirs at thirty-five. Do you get the feeling that God is playing a practical joke?

☎ .... **Rita Rudner**

Cosmopolitan magazine says that a man reaches his sexual peak at eighteen, but a woman doesn't reach hers until thirty-five. Of course, we're not talking age, we're talking minutes.

☎ .... **Traci Skene**

I was with this girl the other night and from the way she was responding to my skill-ful caresses, you would have sworn that she was con-scious, from the top of her head to the tag on her toes.

☎ .... **Emo Philips**

You know what I say about edible panties? I say if you're drunk enough, and your teeth are sharp enough, *every* panty is edible.

☎ .... **Brian McKim**

My girlfriend always laughs during sex, no matter what she's reading.

☎ .... **Emo Philips**

If her lips are on fire and she trembles in your arms, forget her. She's got malaria.

☎ .... **Jackie Kannon**

They say the best exercise takes place in the bedroom. I believe it, because that's where I get the most resistance.

☎ .... **Jeff Shaw**

I love the lines the men use to get us into bed. "Please, I'll only put it in for a minute." What am I, a microwave?

☎ . . . . **Beverly Mickins**

It's okay to laugh in the bedroom so long as you don't point.

☎ . . . . **Will Durst**

This is true, my boyfriend actually called me by another woman's name in bed! I confronted him, "Who's Oprah?"

☎ . . . . **Jennifer Siegal**

Sex after a fight is often the best there is, which is why you're never allowed in the locker room right after a prizefight.

☎ . . . . **Jay Leno**

It's so long since I've had sex, I've forgotten who ties up whom.

☎ . . . . **Joan Rivers**

Ladies, sexually, if your man won't do it, his best friend will.

☎ . . . . **Lewis Ramey**

Did you hear about those two strangers who were arrested for having sex in first class on American Airlines? You know who I feel sorry for? The guy in the middle seat.

☎ . . . . **Jay Leno**

In 1962 all the expression "safe sex" meant was that you move the bed away from the wall so you wouldn't bang your head.

☎ . . . . **David Letterman**

I went to a meeting for premature ejaculators. I left early.

☎ . . . . **Red Buttons**

I had sex for five hours once, but four and a half was apologizing.

☎ . . . . **Conan O'Brien**

I asked my wife, "On a scale of one to ten, how do you rate me as a lover?" She said, "You know I'm no good at fractions."

☎ . . . . . **Rodney Dangerfield**

Engaged women have sex 2.9 times a week. And the .9 is really frustrating.

☎ . . . . **Jay Leno**

I don't think I'm good in bed. My husband never said anything, but after we made love he'd take a piece of chalk and outline my body.

☎ . . . . **Joan Rivers**

When you've been married a long time, sex is like a kite that will only fly when you run with it. Sometimes my wife spices up our marriage—candlelight, massage, incense—it's great, but I'm almost embarrassed. "All this for me?" It's like a chef making sauces, and firing up a little weenie.

☎ . . . . **Danny Liebert**

I don't need Viagra. I need a pill to help me talk afterwards.

☎ . . . . **Garry Shandling**

A new study found that one in five hundred men will die from having sex. That's why we rush through it; we might die!

☎ . . . . **Jay Leno**

Sex Changes

San Francisco will pay for city employees to have sex-change operations. The actual figures are, male-to-female $37,000 and female-to-male $77,000. So you know what every guy is thinking, "I'm walking around with forty grand in my pants."

☎ . . . . **Jay Leno**

One company has installed a third restroom for a trans-sexual employee. The employee leaves the toilet seat halfway up.

☎ . . . . **Craig Kilborn**

A man in Iran had a sex change, and now he wants it reversed. As a woman he can't work or even go out in public alone. However, riding a camel is now way more comfortable.

☎ . . . . **Bill Maher**

Did you read about the Hungarian couple planning simultaneous sex change operations? They've been using too much Calvin Klein's Obsession.

☎ . . . . **Jay Leno**

Sexual Harassment

Mitsubishi Motors had to pay a record thirty-four million dollars to settle a sexual harassment suit brought by female employees, and they still don't get it. Like the other day, they said they got a bad break in the case because the judge was a chick.

☎ .... Jay Leno

Shallowness

There's nothing wrong with being shallow as long as you're insightful about it.

☎ .... Dennis Miller

Shopping

Most men hate to shop. That's why the men's department is usually on the first floor of a department store, two inches from the door.

☎ .... Rita Rudner

I love to go shopping. I love to freak out salespeople. They ask me if they can help me, and I say, "Have you got anything I'd like?" They ask me what size I need, and I say, "Extra medium."

☎ .... Steven Wright

Some women hold up dresses that are so ugly, and they always say the same thing: "This looks much better on." On what? On fire?

☎ .... Rita Rudner

One relatively recent innovation in car buying is haggle-free pricing. They use this system with Saturns. And you know why? Because no one wants to buy a Saturn.

☎ . . . . **Dennis Miller**

Stanford University has developed a drug to cure compulsive shoppers. No matter what you buy, it makes your ass look big.

☎ . . . . **Jay Leno**

Buying something on sale is a very special feeling. The less I pay for something the more it is worth to me. I have a dress I paid so little for that I am afraid to wear it. I could spill something on it, and then how would I replace it?

☎ . . . . **Rita Rudner**

My husband takes me to Home Depot, I want to go home. "It's an entire aisle of nails! Get a sharp one, let's go!"

☎ . . . . **Maryellen Hooper**

I met this wonderful girl at Macy's. She was buying clothes and I was putting Slinkies on the escalator.

☎ . . . . **Steven Wright**

Every town has the same two malls: the one white people go to, and the one white people used to go to.

☎ . . . . **Chris Rock**

Kmart has declared bankruptcy, due to its two closest competitors, Goodwill and the Salvation Army.

☎ . . . . **Jay Leno**

Sin

Lust, pride, sloth, and gluttony, or, as we call them these days, "getting in touch with your sexuality," "raising your self-esteem," "relaxation therapy," and "being a recovered bulimic."

☎ . . . . **P. J. O'Rourke**

Singlehood

I'm single by choice. Not my choice.

☎ . . . . **Orny Adams**

I need a woman. I've been single so long I opened my refrigerator this morning and Mrs. Butterworth looked good to me.

☎ . . . . **Dobie Maxwell**

My family is crazy. I'm single and they're trying to fix me up with the butcher, "C'mon, we'll get free chicken cutlets!"

☎ . . . . **Tracy Esposito**

Being married or single is a choice we all have to make. It's not a great choice; it's sort of like when the doctor goes, "Ointment, or suppositories?"

☎ . . . . **Richard Jeni**

Why get married and make one man miserable, when I can stay single and make thousands miserable?

☎ . . . . **Carrie Snow**

Sleep

I can remember the first time I had to go to sleep. Mom said, "Steven, time to go to sleep." I said, "But I don't know how." She said, "It's real easy. Just go down to the end of tired, and hang a left." So I went down to the end of tired, and just out of curiosity I hung a right. My mother was there, and she said, "I thought I told you to go to sleep."

☎ . . . . **Steven Wright**

Naps are wonderful, aren't they? Sometimes I have to take a nap to get ready for bed.

☎ . . . . **Marsha Warfield**

I was sleeping the other night—alone, thanks to the exterminator.

☎ . . . . **Emo Philips**

Interior Secretary Gail Norton released five condors into the wild today. And then yelled, "Pull!"

☎ . . . . **Jay Leno**

God help me. I'm so tired. I need my sleep. I make no bones about it. I need eight hours a day, and at least ten at night.

☎ . . . . **Bill Hicks**

It turns out that sleeping less leads to big guts on men. So when a man is napping on the couch, he can tell his wife he's working out.

☎ . . . . **Jay Leno**

I read an article in *Self* magazine that said "drunk sleep" isn't really sleeping. If that's the case, I haven't really slept since high school.

☎ . . . . . . Christine O'Rourke

Smoking

I'm not really a heavy smoker anymore. I only get through two lighters a day now.

☎ . . . . Bill Hicks

I tell you I don't get no respect. Why, the surgeon general, he offered me a cigarette.

☎ . . . . . Rodney Dangerfield

A jury awarded twenty million dollars to a woman dying of lung cancer, even though she started smoking after the warning label was added. In the seventies, warning labels were less specific: "Have a nice cancer, Surgeon General." The jury settled on twenty million dollars, rather than a billion, because they were afraid the tobacco companies would run out of money before they themselves got cancer.

☎ . . . . Jon Stewart

Tobacco companies will stop at nothing to win the tobacco wars. Now their scientists are saying some of the smoking research data is no longer valid, because the rats have to step outside their mazes to smoke.

☎ . . . . Dennis Miller

A cigarette company is coming out with a mint that has as much nicotine as a cigarette. Great. Now we can die from secondhand breath as well. The mints are called Life Takers.

☎ .... Jay Leno

Soup

Ever notice that Soup for One is eight aisles away from Party Mix?

☎ .... Elayne Boosler

Wayne Gretzky is the first person on a can of Campbell's Soup. That makes sense, to put a hockey player on a can of soup. It's probably the only thing you can eat without teeth.

☎ .... Jay Leno

Sperm Banks

For a woman the worst thing about a sperm bank is that sperm is no longer free. Just go into a bar, and a sperm container will try to pick you up.

☎ .... Tina Georgie

I know that some lesbians are getting pregnant by going to sperm banks. I couldn't do that. I'm exactly like my grandmother, "What? Everything's frozen! Nothing's fresh?"

☎ .... Judy Carter

Women are removing sperm from the bodies of their dead husbands. Kind of ironic. When they're alive, most men can't give it away.

☎ .... Jay Leno

Sports

Every time a baseball player grabs his crotch, it makes him spit. That's why you should never date a baseball player.

☎ . . . . **Marsha Warfield**

I failed to make the chess team because of my height.

☎ . . . . **Woody Allen**

Can't we silence those Christian athletes who thank Jesus whenever they win, and never mention His name when they lose? You never hear them say, "Jesus made me drop the ball," or "The good Lord tripped me up behind the line of scrimmage."

☎ . . . . **George Carlin**

A couple in Corpus Christi, Texas, named their son "ESPN" after the sports channel. The parents said the boy is okay with his name, but he's very jealous of his baby brother, "ESPN2."

☎ . . . . **Conan O'Brien**

Wayne Gretzky is a national icon in his native Canada, where hockey is a way of life that keeps young people away from drugs, crime, and forming Loverboy.

☎ . . . . **Jon Stewart**

In Russia, if a male athlete loses, he becomes a female athlete.

☎ **Yakov Smirnoff**

How come women don't play ice hockey? Millions of girls played field hockey, and God knows women can skate. Maybe it's the teeth. Women have this vain silly thing about losing their front teeth.

☎ . . . . **Danny Liebert**

Some parents got into a brawl at their kids' soccer match in New Jersey. They said they were just teaching their children European soccer.

☎ . . . . **Craig Kilborn**

Men hate to lose. I once beat my husband at tennis. I asked him, "Are we going to have sex again?" He said, "Yes, but not with each other."

☎ . . . . **Rita Rudner**

In Brazil, a soccer player got in a lot of trouble because during a game he celebrated scoring a goal by taking off all of his clothes. Official said it's bad enough that the player was nude, but then he violated soccer rules by using his hands.

☎ . . . . **Conan O'Brien**

Swimming isn't a sport. It's just a way to keep from drowning. Riding a bus isn't a sport; so why should sailing be a sport? Tennis is just Ping-Pong while standing on the table.

☎ . . . . **George Carlin**

The most favorite activity of nudists: volleyball. The least favorite: dodge ball.

☎ . . . . **Jay Leno**

I like to skate on the other side of the ice.

☎ .... **Steven Wright**

Women play for the reason male athletes used to play: the love of the game. When I read about male professional athletes being arrested for murder, assault, rape, and theft, I agree with those who say they just can't see women competing on the same level as men anytime in the near future.

☎ .... **Dennis Miller**

Statisticians

Definition of a statistician: a man who believes figures don't lie but admits that under analysis some of them won't stand up either.

☎ .... **Evan Esar**

Status

Never keep up with the Joneses. Drag them down to your level; it's cheaper.

☎ .... **Quentin Crisp**

Stocks

The Easter Bunny was hurt in the stock market crash. Yep, all his eggs were in one basket.

☎ .... **Jay Leno**

Jenny Craig plans to go public. Experts expect the stock to start at 150, drop to 90, then drop to 80, get dumped by its boyfriend, and shoot back up to 150.

☎ . . . . **Craig Kilborn**

Styrofoam

After they make Styrofoam, what do they ship it in?

☎ . . . . **Steven Wright**

Success

The road to success is always under construction.

☎ . . . . **Lily Tomlin**

All you need is ignorance and confidence, and then success is assured.

☎ . . . . **Mark Twain**

Suicide

I tried to hang myself with a bungee cord. I kept almost dying.

☎ . . . . **Steven Wright**

Super Heroes

I liked Batman when I was growing up, because he was the only realistic super hero. No super powers, Batman just bought a bunch of cool stuff. The moral of every Batman cartoon? Rich people win. To me, that says a lot more about truth, justice, and the American way than Superman.

☎ . . . . **Brian Dowell**

Surveys

USA Today has come out with a new survey: Apparently three out of four people make up 75 percent of the population.

☎ .... **David Letterman**

I was watching the news and they had one of those polls where you call in and vote on an issue, "Yes," "No," or "Undecided," which caught 6 percent of the vote. This means that there are people in this country who'll take time and spend money to call and tell us they can't make up their mind.

☎ .... **Dennis Regan**

Another study that says 25 percent of people use television to enhance their love life. Unfortunately for the remaining 75 percent, TV *is* their love life.

☎ .... **Jay Leno**

A recent study shows that 75 percent of the body's heat escapes through the head. I guess that means you could ski naked if you had a good hat.

☎ .... **Jerry Seinfeld**

According to a recent survey, men say the first thing they notice about women is their eyes. And women say the first thing they notice about men is they're a bunch of liars.

☎ .... **Jay Leno**

Swimming

I discovered I scream the same way whether I'm about to be devoured by a great white, or if a piece of seaweed touches my foot.

☎ . . . . Kevin James

The swim team at a high school in Darwin, Australia, has a little extra incentive to swim faster, as their unorthodox coach is motivating them by putting a crocodile in the pool. The presence of the croc has shaved 10 percent off each swimmer's personal best, and also raised the urine content of the pool 8,000 percent.

☎ . . . . Craig Kilborn

I always use the buddy system when I'm swimming. I use a buddy chubbier than I am, to keep the sharks away from me.

☎ . . . . Jay Leno

Tattoos

I'm turned on by tattooed women. "What's that on your shoulder? A soy bean? I thought it was a Rice Krispie, but that would be ridiculous."

☎ . . . . Todd Barry

Taxes

You don't pay taxes; they *take* taxes.

☎ . . . . Chris Rock

I wouldn't mind paying taxes, if I knew they were going to a friendly country.

☎ . . . . **Dick Gregory**

Tax day is the one time when crazy irate customers out-number crazy irate postal employees.

☎ . . . . **Jay Leno**

All the big corporations depreciate their possessions, and you can, too, provided you use them for business purposes. For example, if you subscribe to the *Wall Street Journal,* a business-related newspaper, you can deduct the cost of your house, because, in the words of U.S. Supreme Court Chief Justice Warren Burger in a landmark 1979 tax decision: "Where else are you going to read the paper? Outside? What if it rains?"

☎ . . . . **Dave Barry**

The IRS is auditing the NRA. I haven't had this much trouble picking sides since the Iran-Iraq war.

☎ . . . . **Bill Maher**

What is the difference be-tween a taxidermist and a tax collector? The taxider-mist takes only your skin.

☎ . . . . **Mark Twain**

When you did your taxes did you check the box to give one dollar to help Jennifer Lopez buy a bra?

☎ . . . . **Jay Leno**

Teachers

Fifty-two teachers in New York City helped kids cheat on their tests so it would look like the teachers had been doing a gooder job than they had. Those who can't do, teach. Those who can't teach, cheat.

☎ .... **Jon Stewart**

I like it in America, because in Japan, teachers are allowed to hit students. My volleyball teacher in high school threw things at me when she was angry. A pen, a cup, a chair. I wish, just for once, she threw something at me that I wanted. Like a really good-looking guy. That could have improved my receiving skills.

☎ .... **Naoko Okamoto**

I had a terrible education. I attended a school for emotionally disturbed teachers.

☎ .... **Woody Allen**

There's always one teacher you had a crush on. For me it's my wife's aerobics instructor.

☎ .... **Brian Kiley**

I was a substitute teacher for a couple of years, and it's a tough job. And apparently not cool to say, "You guys work on your math problems. If you have any questions, wake me up."

☎ .... **Adam Gropman**

Telemarketing

A suicide hotline is where they talk to you until you don't feel like killing yourself. Exactly the opposite of telemarketing.

☎ . . . . **Dana Snow**

I hate phone solicitors. I'd rather get an obscene call; at least they work for themselves.

☎ . . . . **Margaret Smith**

Telephones

The cell phone people say there's absolutely no danger from cell phone radiation. Boy, it didn't take those tobacco executives long to find new jobs, did it?

☎ . . . . **Bill Maher**

Cordless phones are great. If you can find them.

☎ . . . . **Glen Foster**

At the end of every year, I add up the time that I've spent on hold and subtract it from my age. I don't count that time as really living. Sometimes I spend what seems like hours on hold only to be mysteriously disconnected. These times are so disturbing that I feel justified in subtracting not only from my age, but also from my weight.

☎ . . . . **Rita Rudner**

Sprint is now offering a service that is "talking e-mail." What is this? Didn't that used to be called a phone call?

☎ . . . . **Jay Leno**

Television

Sure, most television nowadays is crap. But guess what? Most television has always been crap. So has most film, music, painting, and literature, ever since the moment mankind starting grinding it out. I'm sure there were cave-wall drawings of dogs playing poker.

☎ . . . . **Dennis Miller**

A&E's *Biography* has been on forever. "This week on *Biography:* Winston Churchill and Mozart." But they're running out of people to profile. Now it's "This week on *Biography:* Captain Crunch and Ann B. Davis."

☎ . . . . **Danny Liebert**

I will never understand why they cook on TV. I can't smell it, can't eat it, can't taste it. The end of the show they hold it up to the camera: "Well, here it is. You can't have any. Goodbye."

☎ . . . . **Jerry Seinfeld**

Ever watch the TV show *Cops*? It's actually a pretty educational show. The most important thing I learned from watching is the one way to avoid being arrested is to wear a shirt.

☎ . . . . **Dennis Regan**

ABC ran a four-hour miniseries on the life of Adolf Hitler. Or, as Pat Buchanan calls it, "Roots."

☎ . . . . **Jay Leno**

Ellen DeGeneres has a new show on CBS. It's called *Not Everybody Loves Raymond*.

☎ .... **David Letterman**

ESPN and Court TV together let me follow the careers of all my favorite athletes.

☎ .... **Jeff Stilson**

Alex Trebek took "Bitter & Jealous for $1,000" when he complained that on *Who Wants to Be a Millionaire* the questions are too easy and Regis Philbin isn't that smart. Trebek, who reads off index cards for a living.

☎ .... **Jon Stewart**

Americans love the Home Shopping Network because it's commercial-free.

☎ .... **Will Durst**

Why would anyone play *Jeopardy* now? Hard questions for $500. On the other shows you can tell how many people are in the Jackson Five for a million.

☎ .... **Chris Rock**

In Russia the big TV show is *Who Wants to Win a Roll of Toilet Paper*. No one's won a whole roll yet.

☎ .... **Jay Leno**

"The Michael Jackson 30th Anniversary Special" aired on CBS. But it's being reported that Michael will have to stop performing live, because he may be losing some body parts during the more rapid dance steps.

☎ .... **Craig Kilborn**

If you don't believe that America is anti-intellectual, than why is it that on *Gilligan's Island* the character who had the worst billing was the Professor?

☎ . . . . **Bill Maher**

I couldn't do a nude scene on TV, because there isn't room.

☎ . . . . **Garry Shandling**

Jerry Springer testified before Chicago's city council. The big issue is whether the fights on his show are real or fake. I hope they're real! Wouldn't it be horrible if those morons on his show weren't actually getting punched in the mouth?

☎ . . . . **Jay Leno**

Oscar winners have been shown to live four years longer than those who are nominated but don't win. And the People's Choice Award still makes a good paperweight.

☎ . . . . **Jon Stewart**

My husband is so confident that when he watches sports on television, he thinks that if he concentrates he can help his team. If the team is in trouble, he coaches the players from our living room, and if they're really in trouble, I have to get off the phone in case they call him.

☎ . . . . **Rita Rudner**

The Jerry Springer Show celebrated its tenth anniversary, so the teenagers on the first show are probably grandparents by now.

☎ . . . . **Conan O'Brien**

It's sweeps again. That's why tonight's news featured "Coeds on Trampolines: How Slowly Can They Eat Bananas?"

☎ . . . . **Jay Leno**

Here's my idea for another one of those "reality based" TV shows: *No Survivors!* One by one, a psychopathic serial killer tracks down and kills all the *Survivor* survivors. Think of it as a public service.

☎ . . . . **George Carlin**

I'm addicted to religious television, I think it's the best entertainment on TV. Televangelists are to me the proof that God exists, and that She has a fantastic sense of humor.

☎ . . . . **Cathryn Michon**

I don't know what's wrong with my television set. I was getting C-SPAN and the Home Shopping Network on the same station. I actually bought a congressman.

☎ . . . . **Bruce Baum**

Nongovernment Iranian TV is now being offered worldwide. The Iranian government gave it two enthusiastic thumbs off.

☎ . . . . **Jon Stewart**

In Russia we only had two TV channels. Channel One was propaganda. Channel Two consisted of a KGB officer telling you, "Turn back at once to Channel One!"

☎ . . . . **Yakov Smirnoff**

Everybody in Los Angeles is in therapy. It's a good thing they don't have parking spaces for the emotionally handicapped. There'd be no place to park.

☎ . . . . **Jackson Perdue**

A man broke a world's record by watching ninety-nine hours of TV. To celebrate, he's going to watch a TV show about Disneyland.

☎ . . . . **Jon Stewart**

Even the best psychiatrist is like a blindfolded auto mechanic poking around under your hood with a giant foam "We're #1" finger.

☎ . . . . **Dennis Miller**

Therapy

A man goes to a psychiatrist: "Nobody listens to me." The doctor says, "Next."

☎ . . . . **Henny Youngman**

After twelve years of therapy my psychiatrist said something that brought tears to my eyes, "*No hablo inglés.*"

☎ . . . . **Ronnie Shakes**

I told my psychiatrist that everyone hates me. He said I was being ridiculous; everyone hasn't met me yet.

☎ ..... **Rodney Dangerfield**

Tickets

I got a jaywalking ticket, which is the dumbest ticket of all. I said, "Is this going to go on my record, or can I go to Walking School and have this taken off?"

☎ .... **Garry Shandling**

In my glove compartment, I had ten moving-violation citations, which are like savings bonds. The longer you keep them, the more they mature.

☎ .... **Bill Cosby**

I went to court for a parking ticket. I pleaded insanity.

☎ .... **Steven Wright**

An airline called Western Pacific is offering round-trip tickets for fifty-nine dollars. The only restriction is that they don't tell you what city you're going to. So basically, you become your luggage.

☎ .... **Jay Leno**

Time

The day after tomorrow is the third day of the rest of your life.

☎ .... **George Carlin**

There's no present. There's only the immediate future and the recent past.

☎ . . . . **George Carlin**

So it is all the same day, the past, the present, and the future existing on the same plane. But you have to change your drawers every couple of hours.

☎ . . . . **Whoopi Goldberg**

Tires

Firestone Tires has put out a pamphlet entitled "Inflate, Rotate, Evaluate." Oddly enough, that's also the title of Britney Spears' autobiography.

☎ . . . . **Jay Leno**

Tools

My husband has to have every tool ever made. "It's an air-compressor. It shoots out air." So does your butt, use that!

☎ . . . . **Maryellen Hooper**

Tornadoes

A tornado touched down, uprooting a large tree in the front yard, demolishing the house across the street. Dad went to the door, opened it, surveyed the damage, muttered, "Damn kids!" and closed the door.

☎ . . . . **Tim Conway**

Toys

Crayons turn out to have had asbestos in them. Kids could draw a house, but not a house on fire.

☎ . . . . **Jon Stewart**

Remember the crayon box with the flesh-colored crayon? Little white kids, "I'm going to draw my mother and father." Black kids, "I don't know nobody looks like this." "Don't throw it out, I can use it to draw the police."

☎ . . . . **D. L. Hughley**

Hasbro introduced a Hispanic G. I. Joe. Not to be outdone, Mattel is introducing "Barbie's Malibu Gardener."

☎ . . . . **Bill Maher**

I went to Toys "R" Us and bought my son a *Jurassic Park* action figure called the Thesaurus. The Thesaurus, if you don't know, was a tiny creature who often used flowery language to extricate himself from potentially life-threatening situations.

☎ . . . . **Dennis Miller**

For $39.95 you can buy the new Cher action figure. It's so lifelike, the breasts, lips, nose, and buttocks are sold separately.

☎ . . . . **Jay Leno**

Trains

This is the thirtieth anniversary of Amtrak, whose motto is "We treat every trip as though it's your last."

☎ . . . . **Jay Leno**

Some people like to travel by train because it combines the slowness of a car with the cramped public exposure of an airplane.

☎ . . . . **Dennis Miller**

Amtrak has unveiled a new train that will travel at 150 mph from New York City to a ditch upstate.

☎ . . . . **Craig Kilborn**

Amtrak says it will now offer online service on its trains. So now not only will the computer crash, but it'll roll down an embankment, too.

☎ . . . . **Jay Leno**

Travel

Travel lets us leave behind our unrealistic prejudices about other places and the people who live there and develop new, more realistic prejudices based on their actual deficiencies.

☎ . . . . **Dennis Miller**

The Bush clan went to Pearl Harbor. It was nice for them to see somebody else getting bombed.

☎ . . . . **Jay Leno**

Last year my friend George and I drove across the country. We switched on the driving, every half mile. We had one tape to listen to the entire trip. I don't remember what it was.

☎ . . . . **Steven Wright**

My husband and I went to Israel, and we took my parents with us, because we felt we don't have enough stress in our lives.

☎ . . . . **Heidi Joyce**

A Dracula convention is an event designed to draw tourists to Transylvania, where, of course, the locals will kill them and suck out all their blood.

☎ . . . . **Jon Stewart**

United States

In Alaska, it's illegal to give an alcoholic beverage to a moose. How lonely are the guys up there? How bad off are you that you've got to get the moose drunk first?

☎ . . . . **Jay Leno**

My parents took me to Amish country, to see a bunch of people that have no cars, no TV, no phone. Who wants to see a whole community that's been grounded? That's the way they should punish kids after they've seen the Amish. "Get up to your room. That's it, I've had it, you are Amish, young man! And don't come down till you've made some noodles and raised a barn."

☎ . . . . **Jerry Seinfeld**

America's one of the finest countries anyone ever stole.

☎ . . . . . . **Bobcat Goldthwait**

I've traveled through the Bible Belt. *Belt* is too narrow a word, I think. It should be "Bible Cummerbund." Or maybe "Bible Body Cast."

☎ . . . . **Sabrina Matthews**

I just heard about the Mercedes back-to-school sale in Beverly Hills.

☎ . . . . **Red Buttons**

I'm concerned about my wife since we moved to California. She's gotten kind of kinky. She likes to tie me up, and then go out with someone else.

☎ . . . . **Tom Dreesen**

I think that's how Chicago got started. A bunch of people in New York said, "Gee, I'm enjoying the crime and the poverty, but it just isn't cold enough. Let's go west."

☎ . . . . **Richard Jeni**

The weekend was hell for me in Connecticut. Other than a circus, what don't you want to have set up around the corner from you on a ninety-five-degree day with no breeze? That's right, a rodeo. And then when you do get a little breeze, "Coming out of chute #2, Widowmaker."

☎ . . . . **David Letterman**

What do you call an Indiana man who becomes a new father? Hoosier Daddy.

☎ . . . . **Jay Leno**

You think New York is bad? You ought to go to Detroit. You can go ten blocks and never leave the scene of the crime.

☎ . . . . **Red Skelton**

> *In the* Detroit Free Press *the mayor of Detroit was quoted as declaring,* "Detroit is God's city." *In a related story, God has moved to the suburbs.*
>
> ☎ **Conan O'Brien**

Houston is talking about keeping Enron's name on its baseball stadium. They should also consider Titanic, Hindenberg, and Custer World.

☎ . . . . **Will Durst**

August I'm in Las Vegas, 120 degrees, but it's a dry heat. That's what they were telling me when they were putting me in the ambulance, "It's a dry heat, Mr. Pinetta."

☎ . . . . **Joe Pinetta**

I just went to Las Vegas in July because I am the stupidest man in the world. People live there, on purpose. What would make anyone start a town in a place that gets to 128 degrees? "Well, we don't have enough fuel to make it to the surface of the sun. Let's live here."

☎ . . . . **Brad Stine**

In my home state of Louisiana we bury the dead above-ground so we can get them to the polls quicker.

☎ . . . . **Leslie Stahl**

The KKK has been dropped from the Adopt a Highway program in Missouri. The Klan would only pick up the white trash.

☎ . . . . **Jay Leno**

Two hundred fifty ferry passengers got stranded for hours in the icy waters just off the coast of New Jersey. When asked to comment, a passenger said, "You know, it's tough. But it could've been worse: We could've made it to New Jersey."

☎ . . . . **Conan O'Brien**

In Seattle you haven't had enough coffee until you can thread a sewing machine while it's running.

☎ **Jeff Bezos**

In New Jersey they have female prisoners answering the tourism hot line. Can't you hear them? "What's your address, and exactly when will you be out of town?" They tell you about New Jersey, and for $2.99 a minute they'll tell you what they'll do to you when you get there.

☎ . . . . **Jay Leno**

Washington, D.C., is to lying what Wisconsin is to cheese.

☎ . . . . **Dennis Miller**

New Hampshire is the last state to accept Martin Luther King Day as a holiday. The state's motto is "Live Free or Die," which appears on license plates made by prisoners.

☎ . . . . **Jon Stewart**

The mayor of New Orleans wants to rename the airport after Louis Armstrong. Naming an airport after a jazz musician? You think flights are late now …

☎ .... **Jay Leno**

Thirty women were arrested for pulling up their blouses in New Orleans. There's a ten-dollar cover charge for the police lineup.

☎ .... **Conan O'Brien**

A man in Utah is in trouble for having five wives. That's what you get in a society without tobacco, alcohol, or porn.

☎ .... **Jon Stewart**

Wisconsin leads the nation in binge drinking, five or more drinks in a single sitting. Or as I call it, brunch.

☎ .... **Jon Stewart**

Vegetarians

A vegetarian is someone who won't eat anything that can have children.

☎ .... **David Brenner**

Not eating meat is a decision; eating meat is an instinct.

☎ .... **Denis Leary**

There are patriotic vegetarians in the American Legion who will only eat animals that were killed in combat.

☎ .... **George Carlin**

I was a vegetarian until I started leaning toward the sunlight.

☎ .... **Rita Rudner**

I tell vegetarians, "Hey, vegetables are living things too. They're just easier to catch."

☎ .... **Kevin Brennan**

I won't eat anything that has intelligence, but I would gladly eat a network executive or a politician.

☎ .... **Marty Feldman**

I'm a Jewish girl raised in a vegetarian family. I'm thinking of opening up my own restaurant soon. I'm gonna call it Soy Veh.

☎ .... **Margot Black**

Viagra

They've renamed Viagra, Ramitall. People have died on Viagra, and they can't close the coffin.

☎ .... **Robin Williams**

Video

If you buy your husband or boyfriend a video camera, for the first few weeks he has it, lock the door when you go to the bathroom. Most of my husband's early films end with a scream and a flush.

☎ .... **Rita Rudner**

Visualization

Visualization is a load of crap. I don't visualize what I don't want, and I have that.

☎ . . . . **Jann Karam**

Voting

A citizen of America will cross the ocean to fight for democracy, but won't cross the street to vote in a national election.

☎ . . . . **Bill Vaughan**

Next time they give you all that civic bullshit about voting, keep in mind that Hitler was elected in a full, free democratic election.

☎ . . . . **George Carlin**

Only 30 percent of Americans vote, and most of them are drunk.

☎ . . . . **Steve Carell**

Voting in this election is like trying to decide which street mime to stop and watch.

☎ . . . . **A. Whitney Brown**

Walking

I was walking down the street. Something caught my eye, and dragged it fifteen feet.

☎ . . . . **Emo Philips**

Watches

Men love watches with multiple functions. My husband has one that is a combination address book, telescope, and piano.

☎ .... **Rita Rudner**

Water

I mix my water myself. Two parts H, one part O. I don't trust anybody.

☎ .... **Steven Wright**

A study shows that bottled water is not any healthier or safer than tap water, leading Beverly Hills residents to buy thousands of bottles of tap water.

☎ .... **Jimmy Fallon**

Weather

On cable TV they have a weather channel, twenty-four hours of weather. We had something like that where I grew up. We called it a window.

☎ .... **Dan Spencer**

I don't understand the terminology on TV weather reports, "The temperature today is twenty-two, but with wind-chill factor, it feels like ten below." What the hell does that mean? Give me something I can use, "The temperature outside is *'Damn!'* But with the wind, it feels more like *'Son-of-a-Bitch!'*" I know how to dress for Son-of-a-Bitch.

☎ .... **Brian McKim**

It was so cold I saw a polar bear wearing a grizzly.

☎ .... **Milton Berle**

It's cold here! So cold that I saw a hot dog vendor putting antifreeze into the water.

☎ .... **David Letterman**

The cold weather is dangerous for women in Los Angeles. At low temperatures, silicone freezes.

☎ .... **Jay Leno**

> *It was so cold out that rap stars were actually chilling out.*
>
> ☎ **Jay Leno**

Russia now has newscasters who appear on TV naked. The weather woman doesn't have to say anything to tell the audience a cold front is coming.

☎ .... **Conan O'Brien**

It was so cold I saw a politician with his hands in his own pockets.

☎ .... **Henny Youngman**

The weather was so bad in Washington that Bob Dole was taking Viagra so rescuers could spot him in the snow.

☎ .... **Jay Leno**

It was so hot today people were thinking of Larry King in a Speedo just for the cold chill it would send down their spines.

☎ .... **Jay Leno**

It was so hot today I went to an ATM machine just to enjoy the feel of a cold gun against the back of my neck.

☎ .... **David Letterman**

It was so hot McDonald's coffee qualified as a cold drink.

☎ .... **Jay Leno**

It always rains on tents. Rainstorms will travel thousands of miles, against prevailing winds, for the opportunity to rain on a tent.

☎ .... **Dave Barry**

Weddings

There are all kinds of magazines for brides, but I think they should have a *Bridesmaid* magazine. With helpful articles like, "Should You Get Drunk and Sleep with the Best Man at the Rehearsal Dinner, or Wait Until After the Ceremony?"

☎ .... **Kelly Maguire**

My fiancé is an atheist, he believes in science, but he wants his belief system reflected in our wedding ceremony. What does that mean: Stephen Hawking will perform the ceremony? "By the power vested in me by the National Academy of Science I pronounce you an inert mass of DNA. You may exchange saliva."

☎ .... **Denise Robb**

Wine

It seems that researchers at Colorado University say wine may help people lose weight. It's not the wine directly that causes the weight loss, it's all the walking around you do trying to find your car.

☎ . . . . **Jay Leno**

Wine, for the very eloquent people, "I don't know whether to have the red wine with the fish or chicken." What's it matter? They're dead! The chicken's not going to reach up from the plate and go, "The red wine!"

☎ . . . . **Robin Williams**

Wal-Mart has its own brand of wine. Now they're one-stop shopping: guns, ammo, and cheap liquor.

☎ . . . . **Jay Leno**

Wal-Mart is coming out with its own wine. Their motto: "We will sell no wine before nine A.M."

☎ . . . . **Craig Kilborn**

Wives

Wives are people who think it's against the law not to answer the phone when it rings.

☎ . . . . **Rita Rudner**

I tell ya, with my wife I got no sex life. Just when I get going, she wakes up.

☎ . . . . . **Rodney Dangerfield**

Tom Green in Utah has five wives. One is the head wife, and I'm not going to comment on that. That's her title. The penalty for five wives is five mothers-in-law.

☎ . . . . **Jay Leno**

Women

Why are *we* wearing makeup? I know a few butt-ugly guys who wouldn't be hurt by a little lip color.

☎ . . . . **Sue Murphy**

Most women are attracted to the simple things in life. Like men.

☎ . . . . **Henny Youngman**

You know what we can be like: See a guy and think he's cute one minute, the next minute our brains have us married with kids, the following minute we see him having an extramarital affair. By the time someone says, "I'd like you to meet Cecil," we shout, "You're late again with the child support!"

☎ . . . . **Cynthia Heimel**

Men say women are too emotional and should be more like them. So I guess the next time I get my heart broken instead of crying and eating a pint of Häagen-Dazs, I should drive recklessly to the nearest bar, get my nose broken, and spend the night in jail, because some guy was *LOOKIN' AT ME*!

☎ . . . . **Kelly Maguire**

A study in the *Washington Post* says that women have better verbal skills than men. I just want to say to the authors of that study, "Duh!"

☎ . . . . **Conan O'Brien**

Most women are introspective, "Am I in love? Am I emotionally and creatively fulfilled?" Most men are outrospective, "Did my team win? How's my car?"

☎ . . . . **Rita Rudner**

Women want men, careers, money, children, friends, luxury, comfort, independence, freedom, respect, love, and three-dollar pantyhose that won't run.

☎ **Phyllis Diller**

Scientists say a woman listens with her whole brain, while a man only listens with half his brain. The other half is picturing her naked.

☎ . . . . **Jay Leno**

Women are successful in the business world because the business world was created by men. Men are babies. And women are good with kids.

☎ . . . . **P. J. O'Rourke**

When a man says "fine," he means everything's fine. When a woman says "fine" she means, "I'm really ticked off, and you have to find out why."

☎ . . . . **John Rogers**

Women cannot complain about men anymore until they start getting better taste in them.

☎ .... **Bill Maher**

Women aren't so hard to understand, they all just want to hear those three little words, "I was wrong."

☎ .... **Reno Goodale**

Women don't want to hear what you think. Women want to hear what they think, in a deeper voice.

☎ .... **Bill Cosby**

If women ran the world we wouldn't have wars. Just intense negotiations every twenty-eight days.

☎ .... **Robin Williams**

Work

Work is the greatest thing in the world, so we should always save some of it for tomorrow.

☎ .... **Don Herold**

I used to work as a temp a lot. And I think there's something about steady exposure to fluorescent lights that can dissolve every trace of a personality.

☎ .... **Laura Kightlinger**

What's an Amish guy with his hand up a horse's ass? A mechanic.

☎ .... **Robin Williams**

I used to work at a factory where they tested cosmetics on animals. But I had to quit because after a while, those bunnies were looking good to me.

☎ . . . . Brian McKim

Never take a job where the boss calls you "babe."

☎ . . . . Brett Butler

I was in a job interview and I said to the guy, "Let me ask you a question. If you're in a spaceship that is traveling at the speed of light, and you turn on the headlights, does anything happen?" He said, "I don't know." I said, "I don't want your job."

☎ . . . . Steven Wright

Most people don't know what they're doing, and a lot of them are really good at it.

☎ . . . . George Carlin

Bring Your Daughter to Work Day is a tradition started twenty years ago by a quick-thinking Ted Kennedy when he was spotted leaving work with an eighteen-year-old.

☎ . . . . David Letterman

Bring Your Dog to Work Day. Do dogs really need to see corporate life? Aren't they already used to sniffing butts?

☎ Jay Leno

World

Argentina had five presidents in two weeks. Why don't they run their elections the way we do here: Count the votes and the guy that loses, wins.

☎ . . . . **Craig Kilborn**

The Australians elected to keep Queen Elizabeth. But they did vote to remove "Island of Drunken Prison Trash" from their flag.

☎ . . . . **Jon Stewart**

Britain is the only country in the world where the food is more dangerous than the sex.

☎ . . . . **Jackie Mason**

Canada is the essence of not being. Not English, not American, it is the mathematic of not being. And a subtle flavor, we're more like celery as a flavor.

☎ . . . . **Mike Myers**

Canada is a country so square that even the female impersonators are women.

☎ . . . . **Richard Brenner**

Canada is an entire country named Doug.

☎ . . . . **Greg Proops**

Canada is a country without a cuisine. When's the last time you went out for Canadian?

☎ . . . . **Mike Myers**

In Cuba the Communist Party will once again allow Christmas to be celebrated there after banning it for thirty years. So if you find yourself shopping for a Christmas gift for someone in Cuba, you can't go wrong with a rubber raft.

☎ . . . . Jay Leno

Fidel Castro celebrated his seventy-fifth birthday. You can tell that he's getting old because he's thinking of retiring and moving to Florida.

☎ . . . . Conan O'Brien

A woman in Iran is running for president. She's a moderate, which in Iran means she just boils the American flag.

☎ . . . . Jay Leno

It's spring in England. I missed it last year; I was in the bathroom.

☎ . . . . Michael Flanders

I moved to France for the smoking, and stayed for the health care.

☎ . . . . David Sedaris

The Germans have cut down trees planted in a swastika formation sixty years ago by a Nazi. Duh. They've left a swastika-shaped hole in the forest.

☎ . . . . Lewis Black

I think we should take Iraq and Iran and combine them into one country and call it Irate. All the pissed-off people live in one place and get it over with.

☎ . . . . Denis Leary

Iran may allow women to remove their veils. For ten minutes a week to brush their teeth and shave.

☎ . . . . **Craig Kilborn**

Iraq has opened an amuse-ment park called Saddam City. Of course, their Tomor-rowland is the fourteenth century.

☎ . . . . **Jay Leno**

In Japan, taking the subway is scary. The platform smells like a dentist's waiting room. The train sounds like that chair the dentist is pumping up. The doors open, that sounds like the straw that sucks up my saliva. I finally get in the train, I'm packed in so close, it feels like the guy next to me is drilling me.

☎ . . . . **Naoko Okamoto**

They've just opened the world's largest roller coaster in Japan. But no one can ride it because the sign says, "You have to be this tall."

☎ . . . . **Craig Kilborn**

North and South Korea are talking reunification. Japan is saying, "Like, I knew you two would get back together."

☎ . . . . **Jon Stewart**

The Middle Eastern states aren't nations, they're quarrels with borders.

☎ . . . . **P. J. O'Rourke**

A meteor landed in the Middle East. Even God is throwing rocks over there.

☎ . . . . **Jay Leno**

Did you see the running of the bulls in Pamplona? I wish those guys would get gored in the groin so they wouldn't be able to pass on the idiocy gene.

☎ . . . . **Jay Leno**

The other day, voters in Paris elected their first openly gay mayor. The new mayor says his first priority is to change the reputation of Parisians from "rude" to "bitchy."

☎ . . . . **Conan O'Brien**

Russia has a serious problem. It seems their population is dying off and they need a dramatic increase in their birth rate immediately. Here's a diplomatic mission that is perfect for Jesse Jackson.

☎ . . . . **Jay Leno**

Instead of going to Pamplona to run with the bulls, I just went into the kitchen and backed into a steak knife.

☎ . . . . **Craig Kilborn**

The way their technology is working lately, the Russians are afraid of being beaten in space by the Amish.

☎ **Jay Leno**

Welcome to ex-Yugoslavia, land of a thousand grievances, where the Christians hate the Muslims, the Serbs hate the Croats, the Bosnians hate the Montenegrins, and everyone has a gun.

☎ . . . . **P. J. O'Rourke**

In the Vatican, I couldn't stop looking at the Sistine Chapel floor. I felt sorry for it. It never gets any attention.

☎ .... **Caryn Leschen**

Yoga

I enjoy yoga. I enjoy any exercise where you get to lie down on the floor and go to sleep.

☎ .... **Rita Rudner**

I started doing yoga. Yoga is a Sanskrit word that means, "Heal your back without health insurance."

☎ .... **Norman K.**

Zoos

A petting zoo is a great place, if you want your kid's clothes to end up inside a goat's stomach.

☎ .... **Bil Dwyer**

Green Room

Veteran funnyman **Joey Adams,** a syndicated comedy columnist, was also the author of twenty-three humor books and hosted various radio and television programs.

Orny Adams can be seen yukking it up at Gotham Comedy Club. Orny's credits include Comedy Central, *Friday Night Videos,* and the *Late Show with David Letterman.*

It was **Charles Addams'** cartoons of a funny and ghoulish family in the *New Yorker* magazine that inspired the Addams family of TV and the movies.

Gracie Allen was a classic comedian whose career ranged from vaudeville and movies to the 1950s sitcom *Burns and Allen.*

Marty Allen is the wiry-haired half of the successful '60s comedy team of Allen & Rossi.

Steve Allen, the bespectacled pioneer of late-night television and a comedian-actor-author who wrote more than four thousand songs, was also the creator of the *Tonight Show* and the *Steve Allen Show.*

Tim Allen is the star of the now-syndicated sitcom *Home Improvement* and movies that include *Toy Story* and *Galaxy Quest.*

Woody Allen is a comedian, actor, and Academy Award–winning director of films that include *Annie Hall* and *Mighty Aphrodite.*

Rabbi **Robert A. Alper** (www.bobalper.com) is the world's only practicing clergyman doing stand-up comedy … intentionally, and author of *Life Doesn't Get Any Better Than This: The Holiness of Little Daily Dramas* and the cartoon book *A Rabbi Confesses.*

Larry Amoros has been featured on HBO's *Young Comedians Special.*

Morey Amsterdam was a classic comedian best known for his role as a comedy writer on *The Dick Van Dyke Show*.

Andy Andrews was voted comedian of the year by the National Association of Campus Activities and entertainer of the year by NACA. His CD is titled *Andy Andrews Live, Caesar's Tahoe*.

Nick Arnette is a comedian, speaker, master of ceremonies, and author of a popular joke book, *The Encyclopedia of Dude*.

Tom Arnold is a comedian and actor who has appeared in the movies *True Lies* and *Nine Months*.

Dave Attell was a writer for *Saturday Night Live*, was nominated for an American Comedy Award, and is the star of Comedy Central's *Insomnia*.

Comedian **Karin Babbitt** teaches acting and stand-up at San Jose State University and is a speaker for Narcotics Anonymous.

Heywood Banks has appeared on A&E's *Evening at the Improv*, MTV's *Half Hour Comedy Hour*, Showtime's *Comedy Club Network*, and the twelfth annual HBO *Young Comedians Special*.

Dave Barry is the author of a gadzillion humor books, including *The World According to Dave Barry*.

Todd Barry has appeared on CBS's *The Late Late Show* and starred in his own Comedy Central special.

Bruce Baum was a regular on ABC's *America's Funniest People* and has appeared numerous times on HBO, Showtime, and Comedy Central.

Gerry Bednob, who likes to be known as the Turban Cowboy, is a favorite on the Vegas circuit and was an international *Star Search* champion.

Comedian **Paula Bell** has appeared on the *Tonight Show* with Jay Leno.

Guy Bellamy is the author of the books *The Comedy Hotel* and *I Have a Complaint to Make*.

Jack Benny was one of the first major radio personalities to make the successful transition to television. *The Jack Benny Program* aired on CBS TV in 1950, became one of early television's most popular shows, and ran for the next fifteen years.

Milton Berle was a classic comedian with numberless appearances on *The Ed Sullivan Show* and the *Tonight Show*.

Shelley Berman is a classic comic who appeared regularly on *The Ed Sullivan Show* and the *Tonight Show* with Johnny Carson.

Sandra Bernhard costarred on *Roseanne* and has starred in a number of films including *The King of Comedy*.

Jeff Bezos is the founder of Amazon.com.

Mike Binder is the star and creator of the HBO series *The Mind of a Married Man*.

Lewis Black is a political correspondent and curmudgeon for *The Daily Show*.

Margot Black is featured on the CD *Comedy Standup Against Domestic Violence*.

Comedian **Chris Bliss** has appeared on the *Tonight Show*.

Comedian **Steve Bluestein** has appeared on *Evening at the Improv* and Comedy Central's *Make Me Laugh*.

Erma Bombeck was a housewife and humorist with dozens of best-selling humor books to her credit.

Elayne Boosler has starred in her own HBO and Showtime specials, including *Party of One*.

In the seventy years he lived in the United States, **Victor Borge**'s unique combination of classical music and humor was displayed on radio, films, television, and Broadway (with *Comedy in Music*, which holds the record for the longest-running one-man show).

Bill Braudis has appeared on *Late Night with Conan O'Brien,* has written for Comedy Central's *Dr. Katz, Professional Therapist,* and is the voice of Doug Savage on the animated series *Science Court*.

Comedian **Kevin Brennan** has appeared on NBC's *Comedy Tonight*.

David Brenner has had a forty-year career in comedy, including a record 158 appearances on the *Tonight Show*.

Steve Bridges has been a featured guest on over one hundred radio stations and performed at the Ice House in Pasadena, the Comedy Store, and the Improv.

Dylan Brody has appeared on A&E's *Comedy on the Road* and FOX TV's *Comedy Express*, written jokes for Jay Leno's *Tonight Show* monologues, and published science fiction and fantasy novels for young adults.

Mel Brooks is a comedian, writer, and director of such films as *Young Frankenstein* and *Blazing Saddles*.

A. Whitney Brown was a host of Weekend Update on *Saturday Night Live* and can be seen on Comedy Central's *Daily Show*.

Roz Browne has appeared on BET's *Comic View*, *The Extreme Gong Show*, and *America's Funniest People*.

Lenny Bruce is the comedian who practically invented comedy plain-speak in the second half of the twentieth century, produced albums including his *Carnegie Hall Concert*, and wrote the book *How to Talk Dirty and Influence People*.

George Burns was a classic comedian whose career stretched from vaudeville to the *Burns and Allen* sitcom and the movie *Oh, God!*

Brett Butler is the star of the syndicated sitcom *Grace Under Fire*.

Comedian **Red Buttons** also won the best supporting actor Golden Globe and Oscar for *Sayonara*.

Steve Carell is a correspondent for *The Daily Show* on Comedy Central.

Drew Carey is, coincidentally enough, the star of *The Drew Carey Show*.

George Carlin has won a Grammy and a CableAce award and was nominated for an Emmy for his comedy albums and HBO and network comedy specials.

Jim Carrey is the star of movies that range from *Dumb and Dumber* to *The Truman Show* and *Man on the Moon*.

Jean Carroll, a classic comedian of the 1950s and 1960s, appeared on *The Ed Sullivan Show* and many other TV programs of the period.

British comedian **Jasper Carrott** has a series of U.K. gold albums to his credit, including *Beat the Carrott* and *The Mole*, as well as the popular TV series *Canned Carrott* and sitcom *The Detectives*.

Johnny Carson hosted NBC's *Tonight Show* for more than thirty years.

Judy Carter is the author of *The Comedy Bible* but bills herself as "just another Jewish lesbian comic-magician."

Dana Carvey was a repertory member of *Saturday Night Live* from 1986 to 1992 who then segued his Garth character into the *Wayne's World* movies.

Comedian **Christopher Case** has also written for the sitcom *Titus.*

Tim Cavanagh is a comedian who has performed for over two hundred corporate groups and is a professional member of the National Speakers Association.

Dick Cavett has parlayed stand-up comedy into his own talk shows on networks, PBS, and cable.

Dave Chappelle is a comedian who has starred in a number of comedy movies, including *Half Baked, Robin Hood: Men in Tights, You've Got Mail,* and *Blue Streak.*

Fran Chernowsky is a freelance paralegal and stand-up comedian.

Anthony Clark is the star of the sitcoms *Yes, Dear* and *Boston Common.*

Comedian **Blake Clark** has guest starred on *Sabrina, the Teenage Witch* as Phil the Dog and on *Spin City, Boy Meets World, The Jamie Foxx Show,* and *Home Improvement.*

Stephen Colbert is a correspondent for Comedy Central's *The Daily Show.*

Scotland's favorite comedian, **Billy Connolly**, has been featured in films, including his star turn in *Her Majesty, Mrs. Brown.*

Tim Conway is a classic comedian best known for his sketch work on *The Carol Burnett Show* and for his Dorf videos.

Pat Cooper is a classic comedian with numerous *Tonight Show* appearances to his credit.

Comedian **Billiam Coronel** has also been a staff writer on the TV series *Men Behaving Badly* and *The Parent 'Hood.*

After having made over thirty national television appearances, **Rick Corso** was selected as one of Showtime's Comedy Club All-Stars and was chosen to be on Comedy Central's *The A-List.*

The title of his first comedy album was prophetic: *Bill Cosby Is a Very Funny Fellow, Right?* This continued to be true during a forty-year career, which includes the 1984–92 TV run of *The Cosby Show* and his books, *Fatherhood* and *Time Flies.*

Aurora Cotsbeck is an Australian actress and comedian who has appeared on the TV series *Stingers* and *Neighbours.*

Comedian **Tom Cotter** has performed on the *Tonight Show.*

Wayne Cotter has appeared on the *Tonight Show* with Jay Leno.

Douglas Coupland is the author of three books, *Generation X, Shampoo Planet,* and, most recently, *Life After God.*

Quentin Crisp was a British wit, raconteur, and author of *The Naked Civil Servant.*

Bill Dana is a classic comic of the 1950s and 1960s best known for his comedy albums featuring the character Jose Jimenez, astronaut.

Michael Dane has been entertaining audiences for fifteen years everywhere from Seattle to Maine as a stand-up comic and with his solo show, *No Apparent Motive,* and he created the Gay and Lesbian Comedy Night at the Comedy Store.

Rodney Dangerfield has starred in the movies *Caddyshack, Back to School,* and improbably enough, *Natural Born Killers* and has won a Grammy for his comedy album *No Respect.*

Ron Darian is a voice actor and writer for the series *7th Heaven.*

Growing up with more than twenty-five cats on a farm in Indiana, it's no wonder that in 1978 **Jim Davis** created the comic strip *Garfield.* The fat, lazy, lasagna-loving, cynical cat appears in over 2,400 newspapers worldwide.

The Dawk is a Los Angeles performer and comedian who has performed on *Soul Train* and at the Hollywood Improv.

Les Dawson was a classic British comic with his own series featured on ITV and the BBC.

Ellen DeGeneres was the groundbreaking star of ABC's *Ellen* and has been featured in movies that include *The Love Letter* and *Mr. Wrong.*

Vance DeGeneres is a sly and witty correspondent for Comedy Central's *The Daily Show.*

Peter De Vries was an American humorist and novelist whose books included *Without a Stitch in Time, Consenting Adults,* and *Comfort Me with Apples.*

Phyllis Diller is a classic comedian who has appeared in a number of movies and dozens of TV shows, including the *Tonight Show.*

Brian Dowell is a Los Angeles–based comedian who has been featured on the sitcom *Titus.*

Tom Dreesen has performed extensively in Las Vegas, on the *Tonight Show,* and as an opening act for Elvis Presley.

Bob Dubac is a comedian who played a heartthrob on the soap opera *Loving.*

Franck Dubosc has performed at the Just for Laughs Montreal Comedy Festival.

Mike Dugan has appeared on the *Tonight Show* with Jay Leno.

Political comedian **Will Durst** is host of the award-winning PBS series *We Do the Work,* taped *One Night Stand* for HBO, and starred in A&E's *A Year's Worth with Will Durst,* which was nominated for a CableAce Award. Durst also has been nominated five times for an American Comedy Award but still hasn't won, making him the Susan Lucci of stand-up.

Leo Dworken is the author of the book *Is Your Dog Jewish?*

Bil Dwyer has appeared on most of the defunct stand-up shows and has had guest-starring roles on *The Larry Sanders Show* and *Ally McBeal.*

Chas Elstner has performed at hundreds of comedy clubs and on *Comic Strip Live,* opened for Gloria Estefan, and appeared on MTV and Showtime.

Evan Esar is the author of the *Comic Dictionary.*

Tracy Esposito has appeared on Louie Anderson's NBC *Comedy Showcase.*

Jimmy Fallon is a *Saturday Night Live* regular and host of Weekend Update.

Marty Feldman was a classic English comedian who appeared in *Young Frankenstein* and other films.

Tina Fey is host of Weekend Update on *Saturday Night Live.*

Totie Fields was one of the top women comedians in the 1950s, and her television appearances included *The Ed Sullivan Show* and the *Tonight Show.*

W. C. Fields is known for his role playing the gravel-voiced, disreputable-looking, rapier-witted misanthrope who loathed children and animals and fought bankers, landladies, and the police in films that include *David Copperfield, My Little Chickadee, and The Bank Dick.*

Carrie Fisher is an actress and writer known for the original *Star Wars* trilogy and her best-selling books *Postcards from the Edge, Surrender the Pink,* and *Delusions of Grandma.*

Greg Fitzsimmons has been featured on the *Tonight Show* and at the Just for Laughs Montreal Comedy Festival.

Michael Flanders is a British comedian who became famous for the show *At the Drop of a Hat;* he made frequent television appearances in the 1950s and 1960s and successfully toured the United States and Canada.

Eric Fleming is a Los Angeles comedian who has performed at the Improv and the Comedy Store.

Glen Foster has been a headliner on the Canadian comedy circuit for over fifteen years and has performed in the United States, Great Britain, and Australia. Glen starred in his own Comedy Network special, *That Canadian Guy,* and has appeared on numerous other TV shows, including CBC's *Comics.*

Jeff Foxworthy is known both for his eponymous sitcom and *You Might Be a Redneck If,* "the biggest-selling comedy album of all time." Foxworthy recently released a new CD, *Big Funny.*

Al Franken has written for and performed on *Saturday Night Live* over several decades and is the author of the books *I'm Good Enough, I'm Smart Enough, and Doggone It, People Like Me!* and *Rush Limbaugh Is a Big Fat Idiot.*

John Frazee of Kingston, New York, won a magazine contest with his theory for producing perpetual motion: Strap buttered toast to the back of a cat.

Sir David Frost has been in the front line of television news and entertainment for over forty years beginning with the satirical news program *That Was the Week That Was* on the BBC in 1962, which was followed by a variety of interview programs in the U.K. and America, broadcast around the world.

Gallagher is the giant-prop comedian known for his numerous Showtime specials, often rerun on Comedy Central.

Janeane Garofalo is the queen of the alternative comedians and an actress who has appeared in films that include *The Truth About Cats and Dogs* and *Mystery Men*.

Tina Georgie has appeared on *The Late Late Show* with Craig Kilborn.

After a lifetime on the stage, actress **Estelle Getty** gained fame at age sixty-one by playing Sophia Petrillo on the sitcom *The Golden Girls*.

Johnnye Jones Gibson works for a newspaper, freelances as a journalist, writes screenplays, and travels the world interviewing and writing newsletters for Anthony Robbins seminars and other events.

"Lonesome" **George Gobel** was the host of the comedy-variety TV series *The George Gobel Show* from 1954 to 1960.

Whoopi Goldberg is the Oscar-winning actress of the film *Ghost*, is cohost of HBO's *Comic Relief*, and has hosted the Oscars and *Hollywood Squares*.

Bob Goldthwait has starred in the movies *Scrooged* and *Shakes the Clown* and on TV series that include the syndicated sitcom *Unhappily Ever After* and *Bobcat's Big Ass Show* on FX.

A touring headliner, **Reno Goodale** has written material for Roseanne and Jay Leno and appeared on HBO, VH-1, and the Comedy Channel.

Classic comedian **Ronnie Graham** was a TV writer and comic songwriter of tunes that include one dedicated to Lizzie Borden, "You Can't Chop Your Mother Up in Massachusetts."

Dick Gregory is a groundbreaking African-American political comedian and civil rights activist, still active in comedy and politics.

Matt Groening is the creator of *The Simpsons*.

Ex-Bostonian **Adam Gropman** is a Los Angeles–based stand-up comic, writer, and actor who contributes to sheckymagazine.com and hollywoodbadass.com.

Mark Gross has appeared on the *Tonight Show*.

Best known for his raunchy Las Vegas routine, **Buddy Hackett** enjoyed substantial Broadway, film, and TV success with such vehicles as *The Music Man, It's a Mad Mad Mad Mad World,* and *The Little Mermaid.*

Rich Hall is a former *Saturday Night Live* cast member and was also a comedy anchor on *Not Necessarily the News.*

Argus Hamilton is a political comedian and *Tonight Show* regular.

Alan Havey has appeared on *Late Night with David Letterman* and in his own Showtime special.

Jim Hayes is a contributor to Laughlines in the *Los Angeles Times.*

Cynthia Heimel is the author of the humor books *Sex Tips for Girls; If You Can't Live Without Me, Why Aren't You Dead Yet?;* and *Advanced Sex Tips for Girls.*

Buck Henry has made lasting contributions to pop culture as co-creator of TV's *Get Smart,* co-scripter of the film *The Graduate,* and as a frequent guest host on *Saturday Night Live.*

Don Herold was a humorist whose work appeared in a number of publications, including *Reader's Digest.*

In the 1980s and early 1990s **Bill Hicks** made eleven appearances on the David Letterman show and released his first concert video, *Sane Man.* Hicks recorded four comedy albums during his lifetime (including *Dangerous* and *Relentless)* and the albums *Arizona Bay* and *Rant in E-Minor,* which were issued posthumously.

Renee Hicks was named the 1995 College Comedian of the Year and has appeared on Comedy Central's *Premium Blend.*

Cullen Hightower has written columns for *Forbes* magazine.

Comedian **Harry Hill** has appeared on the *Late Show with David Letterman.*

Stephanie Hodge is the star of the syndicated sitcom *Unhappily Ever After.*

Daryl Hogue is a comedian and voice-over talent who has been featured in commercials for 7-Eleven, Ford, and Hewlett Packard.

Maryellen Hooper won an American Comedy Award, and her numerous television appearances include the *Tonight Show* and her own Comedy Central *Lounge Lizards* special.

Bob Hope is a classic comedian whose career ranged from vaudeville to the series of *Road* movies with Bing Crosby and innumerable television specials.

Kin Hubbard was an American journalist, humorist, homespun philosopher, and columnist for the *Indianapolis News*.

Coincidentally enough, **D. L. Hughley** is the star of the ABC sitcom *The Hughleys*.

Dom Irrera hosted Showtime's *Full Frontal Comedy* and won an American Comedy Award.

Eddie Izzard is the British transvestite and stand-up comedian who starred in his own 1999 HBO special and movies that include *Mystery Men*.

Sally Jackson is an actress and comedian who has performed at the Improv and Comedy Store in Hollywood. Her film and TV credits include *Natural Born Killers* and *Judging Amy*.

On his very own sitcom, **Kevin James** is *King of Queens*.

Michael Jeffreys is a speaker and author of four books, including his latest, *Success Secrets of the Motivational Superstars*.

Richard Jeni has been rewarded for his comic fluidity with two CableAce Awards and one American Comedy Award.

Geri Jewell has appeared on *Girls Night Out* and *Comic Strip Live* and was a recurring character on the sitcom *Facts of Life*.

Penn Jillette is the talking half of the comedy magician duo Penn and Teller.

Diana Jordan was an American Comedy Awards nominee, appeared in the movie *Jerry Maguire*, and is the author of the book *Women Are from Venus, Men Are from Uranus*.

Heidi Joyce has appeared on the CBS special *Everybody Loves Raymond's Ray Day*, opened for Melissa Manchester in Las Vegas, and is the star and producer of the CDs *Comedy Standup Against Domestic Violence*, Volumes 1 and 2.

Norman K. (normank_comic@hotmail.com) performs at clubs in the New York area.

Jackie Kannon is a classic comedian whose record albums include *Live from the Ratfink Room* and *Songs for the John*.

Jann Karam has appeared on *Politically Incorrect*, the *Tonight Show*, *Evening at the Improv*, and Lifetime's *Girls Night Out*.

Jonathan Katz played doctor on Comedy Central's *Dr. Katz, Professional Therapist* and is the author of *To Do Lists of the Dead*.

Margo Kaufman was an American humorist whose books include *This Damn House!* and *1-800-Am-I-Nuts?*

Patrick Keane has appeared at the Irvine Improv, the Comedy Store, Mixed Nuts, the Ha Ha Café, and other comedy venues throughout Southern California.

Comedian **Tom Kearney** also does voice-overs, has appeared in many commercials and won leading roles in several independent films including *Fruit of the Vine* and *The Flipside*.

Garrison Keillor is host of NPR's *Prairie Home Companion* and author of the book *Lake Wobegon Days*.

Bobby Kelton has appeared on the *Tonight Show* and the *Late Show with David Letterman*.

Maura Kennedy is an actress and comedian who has appeared on the sitcom *Cybill*, is a recurring character on *Days of Our Lives*, and was a quarter-finalist in Ed McMahon's *Next Big Star*.

Tom Kenny has appeared on NBC's *Comedy Tonight*.

Jean Kerr was a humor writer best known for her book *Please Don't Eat the Daisies*.

In addition to being the comedy Queen of Sardonica, **Laura Kightlinger** is one of Comedy Central's *Pulp Comics*.

Craig Kilborn is the host of CBS's *The Late Late Show*.

Brian Kiley is an Emmy-nominated writer who appears regularly on the *Tonight Show* and *Late Night with Conan O'Brien*.

Andy Kindler has appeared on *Late Night with David Letterman* and is a regular performer on *Everybody Loves Raymond*.

Bill Kirchenbauer was featured in *Growing Pains* and starred in the sitcom *Just the Ten of Us*.

Robert Klein is a comedian who has segued from best-selling 1970s comedy albums to performing in a number of movies including *The Landlord* and a recurring role on the TV series *Sisters*.

Sue Kolinsky has performed on the *Tonight Show* and many other comedy shows.

Jared Krichevsky is an eighteen-year-old actor on the stage and in commercials, on both radio and TV, as well as a comedian who has performed at the Comedy Store.

Comedian **Cathy Ladman** has appeared on the *Tonight Show* a bazillion times, was a recurring neighbor on *Caroline in the City*, and has appeared on *Just Shoot Me*.

Denis Leary has starred in his own HBO specials, a number of films including *The Ref* and *Two if by Sea*, and the ABC show *The Job*.

Okay, she's not a comedian, but **Fran Lebowitz** is the incisively witty author of best-selling humor books including *Metropolitan Life*.

Robert G. Lee can be seen on the religious game show *Inspiration Please* on the Faith and Values network.

Carol Leifer was a producer on *Seinfeld* and the star of her own sitcom, *Alright Already*.

Jay Leno is host of NBC's *Tonight Show*.

Caryn Leschen is a cartoonist, illustrator, and comedy writer best known for her advice comic, *Ask Aunt Violet* (www.auntviolet.com).

David Letterman is the host of CBS's *Late Show*.

Sam Levenson was a beloved American humorist whose books include *In One Era and Out the Other* and *You Don't Have to Be in Who's Who to Know What's What*.

Joe E. Lewis was a comedian and singer in the 1920s, when mobsters cut his throat. Lewis survived and returned to stand-up comedy, where he flourished from the 1940s through the 1960s, appearing frequently in Las Vegas. Frank Sinatra starred in a movie based on Lewis' life, *The Joker Is Wild*.

In addition to his numerous HBO specials, **Richard Lewis** has starred in the sitcom *Anything But Love* and in the Mel Brooks movie *Robin Hood: Men in Tights*.

Danny Liebert is a best-selling bumper sticker writer ("Jesus Is Coming— Look Busy") who has segued into performing comedy at the Comic Strip, Standup NY, Caroline's, and numerous more ephemeral venues.

Penelope Lombard has appeared on Comedy Central's *Premium Blend*.

Al Lubel has performed on *Evening at the Improv and Comic Strip Live* and has been a featured patient on Comedy Central's *Dr. Katz*.

Cecile Lubrani is an actress and comedian who has performed at the Comedy Store and the Improv in Hollywood.

Daniel Lybra is a Roundtable Comedy Conference Award–winning comedian and comedy writer.

Norm Macdonald has showcased his wry smirk as a stand-up and as anchor on *Saturday Night Live*, which was followed by the eponymous smirk sitcom *Norm*.

Don MacLean is a British comedian with a slew of British TV and radio credits.

Kathleen Madigan won an American Comedy Award for Best Female Stand-up and starred in her very own HBO *Comedy Half Hour*.

Kelly Maguire is an actress and comedian who has performed at the Comedy Store and the Improv in Hollywood, participated in the Aspen Comedy Festival, and won a Dramalogue award for Best Actress. Her recent film credits include *Stranger in My House* for Lifetime television.

Bill Maher is the host of ABC's *Politically Incorrect*.

Comedian **Henriette Mantel** has appeared in *The Brady Bunch Movie, A Very Brady Sequel,* and *The Animal*.

Jeff Marder, a seasoned stand-up comedian and television game show host, helped create the computer game Sklif's Attitude.

Melissa Maroff is a Los Angeles–based comedian and the second-place winner of the Far Rockaway Trivia contest.

Judith Martin is the amusing etiquette columnist whose books include *Miss Manners' Guide to Domestic Tranquillity* and *Miss Manners' Guide to Excruciatingly Correct Behavior.*

Steve Martin is a comedian who has starred in and directed such comedy films as *The Jerk* and *Bowfinger.*

Groucho Marx was a comedian who, with the Marx Brothers, made a number of the funniest films of the 1930s, including *Duck Soup,* and whose marvelous 1950s game show, *You Bet Your Life,* still deserves viewing on some cable channel smart enough to feature it.

Jackie Mason is a forty-year comedy veteran and the star of several one-man Broadway shows, including *The World According to Me.*

Kate Mason is a comedian who plays clubs and colleges everywhere.

Sabrina Matthews has been featured on Comedy Central's *Out There in Hollywood* and performed at the Montreal Just for Laughs Festival.

Dobie Maxwell has had an amazing life. His parents were bikers, and his best friend since childhood robbed a bank *twice* and tried to blame the second robbery on Dobie. Despite that, Dobie Maxwell has survived to become a morning radio host and comedian who headlines across America.

Kris McGaha is the Excess Hollywood correspondent on NBC's *Tonight Show* and has appeared in NBC's *Comedy Showcase,* HBO's *Curb Your Enthusiasm,* and in the film *Following Tildy.*

Paul McGinty has been an actor, a comedy radio show host, a stand-up comic, and a cutup at the dinner table as a kid.

Steve McGrew is a veteran of virtually every cable comedy show, including *Evening at the Improv, Caroline's Comedy Hour, Comedy on the Road from London,* MTV, VH-1, TNN, and *Star Search.*

Brian McKim is a writer and a stand-up comic who is also the editor and publisher of SHECKYmagazine.com.

John Mendosa has appeared on the *Tonight Show* and is one of Showtime's *Pair of Jokers.*

Cathryn Michon is the host of AMC's *The Grrl Genius Club.* She has written for a number of TV series and is author of the book *The Grrl Genius Guide to Life.*

Comedian **Beverly Mickins** has appeared on Lifetime's *Girls Night Out*, in *Thirtysomething,* and in the movie *Steel and Lace.*

Bette Midler is the comedy diva who has appeared in movies ranging from *Beaches* to *The First Wives Club.*

Dennis Miller is the possessor of a God-given sarcasm and the star of HBO's *The Dennis Miller Show.*

Larry Miller is featured in both of the *Nutty Professor* movies and played the pregnancy-obsessed father of teenagers in *Ten Things I Hate About You.*

Spike Milligan is the favorite comic of Prince Charles and, when presented with a British Comedy Award for Lifetime Achievement, famously rewarded the prince by calling Charles "a groveling little bastard" on live TV.

Comedian **Jay Mohr** has starred in several films, including *Jerry Maguire* and *Paulie.*

Corbett Monica appeared eighteen times on *The Ed Sullivan Show* and had frequent guest stints on the *Tonight Show* with Johnny Carson. Monica spent forty years as the opening act for Frank Sinatra and other big-name singers, and he appeared in the film *Broadway Danny Rose* and the TV sitcom *Get Smart.*

Kelly Monteith has appeared on Comedy Central's *The Daily Show.*

Dudley Moore was the diminutive, quick-witted performer who teamed up with fellow Oxford graduates to create the satirical revue *Beyond the Fringe.* Moore and colleague Peter Cook went on to make the movie *Bedazzled,* and in the 1980s Moore became an unlikely Hollywood star with his performances in *10* and *Arthur.*

Eric Morecambe and **Ernie Wise** became the popular stars of a long-running British TV series. *The Morecambe and Wise Show* first appeared in 1961 and led to a number of guest appearances in the United States on *The Ed Sullivan Show* and in three feature films.

François Morency has been featured at the Just for Laughs Montreal Comedy Festival.

Martin Mull is a comedian and actor whose TV appearances range from *The Smothers Brothers Comedy Hour* and the *Tonight Show* to the role of the gay boss on *Roseanne.*

Sue Murphy was the star of her own Comedy Central special.

Robert Murray is a software engineer and comedian who has performed in many venues throughout Southern California.

Kevin Nealon is a headlining comedian, actor, and one of the longest-running cast members of *Saturday Night Live.*

Irit Noy is a comedian and actress who has appeared at the Improv in Hollywood.

Buzz Nutley *(www.buzznutley.com)* is a professional comedian who has written for the *Pittsburgh Post Gazette* and *Los Angeles Times,* sold material to Jay Leno and Yakov Smirnoff, and opened for Jon Stewart.

Conan O'Brien, a former writer for *Saturday Night Live* and *The Simpsons,* is the host of the NBC talk show *Late Night.*

Naoko Okamoto was born and raised in Yokohama, Japan. She came to the United States so she could say thank you and "You are the coolest people in the world!" out loud to her family, relatives, and friends who love her. The prize In the Cracker Jack box was that she met her husband.

Robert Orben is the author of the *Speaker's Handbook of Humor.*

Christine O'Rourke is a screenwriter and comedian who has performed at the Improv in Hollywood.

P. J. O'Rourke is a humorist, satirist, and author of books that include *Modern Manners* and *Eat the Rich.*

Patton Oswalt has been seen on *Seinfeld* and is a cast member of CBS's *King of Queens.*

Cheri Oteri is a cast member of *Saturday Night Live.*

Guy Owen has been a comedian and motivational and conference speaker for over twenty years and has performed at the Comedy Store, for President and Mrs. Carter, and in commercials for Honda and Black and Decker

Dorothy Parker was a humorist, short story writer, and screenwriter whose credits include the original *A Star Is Born.*

Pat Paulsen was a comedian featured on the groundbreaking *Smothers Brothers Show* who satirically ran for president for three decades.

Jackson Perdue is a casino favorite in Las Vegas and Tahoe and has appeared on the Playboy Channel.

Emo Philips has appeared on numerous HBO and Showtime specials, as well as in the "Weird" Al Yankovic movie *UHF*.

John Pinette has appeared on Comedy Central's *Dr. Katz, Professional Therapist*.

Marilyn Pittman has been featured in the videos *All Out Comedy* and *Out for Laughs*, in the books *A Funny Time to Be Gay* and *Revolutionary Laughter,* and in the movie *EdTV,* and is a commentator for NPR station KQED in San Francisco.

Paula Poundstone has starred in a number of her own HBO comedy specials.

In addition to having been one of the frightfully inventive stars of Comedy Central's *Whose Line Is It Anyway,* **Greg Proops** has been the host of the game shows *Vs* and *Rendez-View*.

Richard Pryor is a nearly forty-year veteran of comedy recording, movies, and TV, including the groundbreaking 1970s *Richard Pryor Show* and the movie *Silver Streak*.

Colin Quinn is a comedian and former anchor of Weekend Update on *Saturday Night Live*.

Steve Race was a BBC Radio disc jockey.

Gilda Radner was one of the original cast members of *Saturday Night Live*.

Lewis Ramey has appeared on Comedy Central's *Premium Blend*.

Bette-Jane Raphael is the author of humorous essays that include "The Myth of the Male Orgasm."

Mitch Ratliffe has written humorously for the *Technology Review* and elsewhere.

Greg Ray has been seen on *Evening at the Improv, P.M. Magazine*, and CNN. But he is perhaps best known for holding the watermelon in the Ginsu knife commercials.

Larry Reeb has appeared on Showtime's *Comedy Club All-Stars* and A&E's *Evening at the Improv*.

Dennis Regan has appeared on the *Tonight Show* with Jay Leno.

Caroline Rhea isn't a witch, but she plays one on the sitcom *Sabrina*.

Andi Rhoads is a Los Angeles comedian who has performed at the Improv and the Comedy Store in Hollywood.

Call out the coincidence police: **Tom Rhodes** was the star of the NBC sitcom *Mr. Rhodes*.

Comedian **Ron Richards** won an Emmy Award for his writing on *Late Night with David Letterman* and a CableAce Award for HBO's *Not Necessarily the News*. He has also been on the writing staff of the *Tonight Show* and NBC's *Saturday Night Live*.

Karen Ripley has been performing as an out lesbian since 1977 and has appeared on Comedy Central's *The Daily Show*.

Joan Rivers is a comedian, actress, talk show host, best-selling author, and commentator for *E! Style*.

Denise Munro Robb has been seen on A&E, Lifetime, Comedy Central, and MTV, and is a political activist who ran for Los Angeles City Council. Robb recently got married and came to the realization that she doesn't need a man in her life to make her happy. She can be miserable either way.

Robin Roberts was a writer and voice performer for the nationally syndicated radio show *Rick Dee's Weekly Top 40* and is the creator of the Los Angeles showcase Comedy by the Book.

Johnny Robish is a comedian whose jokes appear frequently in the Laugh Lines column of the *Los Angeles Times,* and whose gigglebytes are featured in the Internet radio program *Radio Free OZ*.

Chris Rock is a comedian and actor who is, natch, host of HBO's *The Chris Rock Show*.

Comedian **John Rogers** holds a graduate degree in physics and served as writer/producer on the hit series *Cosby*.

Will Rogers was a favorite American comedian and humorist whose career spanned from the Ziegfield Follies through vaudeville and the movies.

Roseanne is a comedian who has specialized in such eponymous TV as *Roseanne,* the sitcom, and *The Roseanne Show,* a talk show.

Mike Rowe has been featured on NBC's *Comedy Showcase*.

Rita Rudner has appeared on the *Tonight Show*, has been featured on any number of comedy specials, including her own on HBO, and is author of the books *Naked Beneath My Clothes* and *Tickled Pink*.

Mark Russell is a political satirist and songwriter with lots of his own PBS specials.

Tom Ryan lives in Los Angeles and has appeared on Comedy Central's *Premium Blend* and NBC's *Late Friday*.

Bob Saget was the star of the sitcom *Full House* and host of *America's Funniest Home Videos*.

In the 1950s, **Mort Sahl** was a groundbreaking political comic who appeared frequently on the *Tonight Show* and continues to provide his sardonic comments onstage.

Adam Sandler is a former cast member of NBC's *Saturday Night Live* and the star of a string of comedy movies, including *Happy Gilmore*, *The Waterboy*, and *The Wedding Singer*.

Mark Schiff performs regularly on the *Late Show with David Letterman* and the *Tonight Show* and has managed to overcome the subject of his Showtime special, *My Crummy Childhood*.

David Sedaris is a humorous commentator on NPR and the author of the book *Me Talk Pretty One Day*.

Jerry Seinfeld helped rethink the sitcom with his eponymous *Seinfeld*.

Six-time Emmy Award winner **Ross Shafer** was a host of *Match Game* and the Miss America Pageant.

Ronnie Shakes was a comedian and TV writer who made frequent appearances on the *Tonight Show*.

Garry Shandling is the star and creator of HBO's *Larry Sanders Show*.

Thom Sharp's bald mug is a TV commercial staple for such products as Goodyear tires and General Electric refrigerators.

Dick Sharples is a British comedian who has written for the TV series *In Loving Memory*.

Jeff Shaw is a freelance humorist and columnist for SHECKYmagazine.com, as well as a comedy club headliner with over four thousand performances to his credit since 1987.

Wil Shriner has performed regularly on the *Tonight Show* and *Late Night with David Letterman*.

Jimmy Shubert was featured at the Just for Laughs Montreal Comedy Festival.

Jennifer Siegal has been a Disneyland portrait artist, dot-com illustrator, and movie critic, and she writes a monthly art column in San Francisco. On weekends, she likes to go where the green lights take her.

Sinbad is the star of the movies *House Guest* and *First Kid* and the HBO movie *The Cherokee Kid*, as well as several HBO comedy specials.

Carol Siskind has appeared on *Evening at the Improv, Girls Night Out, Comedy on the Road,* and innumerable other comedy specials.

Red Skelton started as a vaudeville performer and worked his way up to *The Red Skelton Show*, which ran on TV for twenty years, from 1951 to 1971.

Traci Skene is a stand-up comic and the co-creator, editor, and publisher of SHECKYmagazine.com.

Comedian **Steve Skrovan** has written for *Seinfeld*.

Yakov Smirnoff emigrated from Russia to entertain in America as a comedian from Las Vegas to the White House. Smirnoff has also appeared in movies that include *Moscow on the Hudson* and in his own TV series, *What a Country*.

Margaret Smith has won an American Comedy Award, was recently featured in her own Comedy Central special, and is one of the stars of *That '80s Show*.

During nearly forty years in comedy, the **Smothers Brothers** have had prime-time comedy series in both the 1960s and 1980s, have done guest appearances on innumerable TV shows, countless engagements as headliners in Las Vegas, and continue to do coast-to-coast concert tours.

Carrie Snow is a stand-up comedian and was a writer on both the *Roseanne* shows.

Dana Snow has been doing stand-up for centuries, and his comedy writing ranges from jokes for Phyllis Diller and other comedians to *The Flintstones* children's books. Two of his movie scripts are currently optioned, including one based on a joke he wrote for Billy Crystal and the 1997 Academy Awards show.

Spanky has appeared on *Evening at the Improv* and Showtime's *Comedy Club Network.*

Winston Spear has been performing in clubs for more than a decade in Canada and the United States, and as far away as the United Arab Emirates, and has been featured on CTV and the Comedy Network's *Comedy Now.*

Dan Spencer appeared in the movie *Shakes the Clown.*

Leslie Stahl is a correspondent and anchor of CBS's 60 *Minutes.*

Tim Steeves has been featured at the Just for Laughs Montreal Comedy Festival.

Barry Steiger has opened on the road for Brett Butler, appeared on the sitcom *Grace Under Fire* and *The Joan Rivers Show,* and began a gay and lesbian comedy night at the Comedy Store in Los Angeles.

Jon Stewart is the host of Comedy Central's *The Daily Show.*

Jeff Stilson has appeared on *Late Night with David Letterman* and was featured in the fourteenth HBO *Young Comedians Show.*

Brad Stine has headlined in forty-eight states, has appeared on MTV, Showtime, and *Evening at the Improv,* and is represented by the Clean Comedians agency.

In addition to founding her own religion (Judyism), comedian **Judy Tenuta** is a panelist on *The Match Game* and star of the film *Butch Camp.*

One of the founding members of SCTV, **Dave Thomas** has also starred in the movies *Strange Brew* and *The Coneheads.*

Lily Tomlin was an original cast member of *Laugh-In,* has acted in such films as *Nashville* and *Orange County,* and appeared in TV series including *Murphy Brown.*

Jill Turnbow has appeared on *Evening at the Improv, Comedy on the Road, Comedy Club Network,* and *Girls Night Out.*

Mark Twain was a humorist and great American novelist whose books include *The Adventures of Tom Sawyer* and *The Adventures of Huckleberry Finn.*

Jeff Valdez has been featured on *Comedy Compadres*.

Matt Vance is the morning show producer for *Mick & Allen's Freak Show* on Rock 99 radio in Salt Lake City.

Bill Vaughan was a columnist for *The Kansas City Star* for over thirty years, and his humor books include *Bird Thou Never Wert* and *Sorry I Stirred It*.

King of the deadpan comics, **Jackie Vernon** made frequent appearances on *The Ed Sullivan Show* and his wry, sad-sack style has influenced many of today's popular comedians. But Vernon may be best known to kids of all ages as the voice of Frosty the Snowman in two animated Christmas specials.

George Wallace is a regular on both the *Tonight Show* and *Late Night with David Letterman*.

Wally Wang is a comedian and an actor who, in his latest performance on the Internet, managed to convince thousands of men that he's a twenty-three-year-old blonde. He has also appeared on A&E's *Evening at the Improv*, performs in Las Vegas, wrote the books *Visual Basic for Dummies* and *Microsoft Office for Dummies*, and publishes a computer humor column in *Boardwatch Magazine*.

Comedian **Marsha Warfield** played bailiff Roz Russell on the sitcom *Night Court* and later joined the cast of *Empty Nest*.

Joel Warshaw has performed for his family and friends for years and now can be seen performing in Los Angeles at the Comedy Store and at the L.A. Cabaret Comedy Club.

Damon Wayans was the star and one of the creators of *In Living Color*, has starred in several movies including *The Last Boy Scout*, and appeared in three of his own HBO specials.

Sheila Wenz has appeared on Lifetime, A&E, and Comedy Central.

Suzanne Westenhoefer was the star of her own HBO special, *Nothing in My Closet but My Clothes*.

Betty White is an actress and comedienne who has starred in classic TV series that include the *Mary Tyler Moore Show* and *The Golden Girls*.

George Will is a columnist for *Newsweek*.

Robin Williams received an Academy Award for *Good Will Hunting* and is the star of dozens of movies including *Mrs. Doubtfire* and *Flubber*, as well as a cohost of HBO's *Comic Relief*.

Tom Wilson has more than fifty films, TV shows, and comedy specials to his credit, including the *Back to the Future* trilogy; the Emmy Award–winning cable film *Andersonville; Sabrina, the Teenage Witch*; and the critically acclaimed *Freaks and Geeks*.

John Wing has been featured at the Just for Laughs Montreal Comedy Festival.

Dennis Wolfberg was a beloved 1980s comedian who was a *Tonight Show* regular and a cast member of the TV series *Quantum Leap*.

Scott Wood's many television credits include ABC, CBS, FOX, *America's Funniest People*, A&E's *Comedy Central* and *Comedy on the Road*, and the Family Channel.

Steven Wright has appeared on numerous HBO specials, was a recurring cast member of *Mad About You*, and received an Oscar nomination for Best Short Film.

Tim Young has performed at over two hundred colleges and was nominated for Comedian of the Year twice. He was a comedic voice on MTV's *Daria* and has appeared on NBC's *Friday Night* and Comedy Central's *Premium Blend*.

Henny Youngman was a classic comedian and king of the one-liners whose career ranged from vaudeville and the Catskills to Johnny Carson's *Tonight Show*.

Peter Zamora has a degree in broadcasting and theater from Columbia University in New York and has appeared in national commercials for Coca-Cola and Disneyland.